# GOOD
## ANSWERS
### TO GOOD QUESTIONS

# GOOD
# ANSWERS
## TO GOOD QUESTIONS

How to confidently answer
50 common questions about the Church

# CHRIS HUSTON

Covenant Communications, Inc.

Printed in the United States of America
First Printing: February 2016

21 20 19 18 17 16      10 9 8 7 6 5 4 3 2 1

ISBN 978-1-68047-667-5

To Mark McDonough, president of the Mississippi Jackson Mission, 2012–2015, whose steady, noble leadership has been an inspiration to all of us called to wear name tags. One night over dinner we discussed how missionaries can respond to difficult questions. "You know," he said, "you really ought to write some of this stuff down." And in that sentence this book was born.

And to my wife, Barbara, whose thoughtful comment, "You could do it kind of like scripture mastery cards," flipped the switch that showed me how to proceed. And, of course, for a million other of her tender mercies that have blessed my life beyond measure.

# TABLE OF CONTENTS

QUESTIONS ABOUT THE BOOK OF MORMON

Part 3: Wise as serpents, harmless as doves; A time to speak, a
     time to keep silence

# INTRODUCTION

Frozen. I couldn't have moved my feet if I'd wanted to.

Worse was the way my mind went to mush. It was like one of those dreams when the easiest task in the world is in front of you, but you can't move, can't speak, can't think.

Meanwhile, she waited with a look of growing disappointment. "I mean, I've heard that you people think you're Christians, but you don't even have a cross on your church. That's just not right."

"Well," I stammered, "it's just not the way we do things. We—"

"I don't see how anyone can call himself a Christian who goes to a church that refuses to have a cross anywhere in sight."

"Well, let me explain a little about the Book of Mormon."

"Don't get me started on that. And that Joseph Smith guy. My pastor told me all about him. And all the wives. No thanks."

And she walked away.

I hung my head. Clearly, I was a failure as a member missionary.

These kinds of gospel smackdowns have occasionally happened to me and perhaps to you. In our hearts, a testimony burns. On Sundays we participate in our classes and share our deepest feelings. We don't know everything about the Church, but we know a lot, and we talk freely with our ward family and friends about what we know. We go home feeling uplifted. And then someone at school or at work or in the grocery store asks us a question, and we turn to stone.

At the time I am writing this, I am serving as a counselor in the full-time mission presidency of the Mississippi Jackson Mission. The mission covers most of Mississippi and the two stakes that cover the northern half of Louisiana. During the time I have served in this calling, I have had the great fortune to associate closely with an inspired mission president and with young missionaries who are courageously serving the Lord. I have also been blessed to work with hundreds of members as we discuss how to break down the barriers that separate us from the humble followers of Christ who surround us but miss the truth because they know not where to find it.[1]

In the process I've learned a great deal about what is and isn't effective in sharing the gospel, particularly when it comes to answering questions from those who are curious about our faith. These pages are a result.

Many of us are defensive about sharing what we know with others, even when we are asked directly. This might happen for a number of reasons:

- We are afraid that we won't do justice to the majesty of the gospel.
- We "freeze" and discover that at the moment of truth we can barely remember our names, let alone where to find Moroni's promise.
- We are afraid that we may be attacked for our deepest beliefs, that others will "tell us what we believe" and then ridicule us.

As a result we tend to see missionary moments not as an opportunity to let our light shine[2] but as a threatening moment where failure seems likely.

We all want to do our best to follow the prophet's call to "hasten the work," but in my experience there's still a lot of fuzziness about our purpose. It's worth asking: *What is our goal?* Many of us still aren't sure—except that we're reasonably certain that if there isn't a baptismal font filling up somewhere next Saturday because of our efforts, we've probably failed. Despite careful instruction, far too many of us still measure our success by the number of people in recent months we have prayed about, befriended, taught, and baptized. Anything less than this leaves us feeling that we have disappointed the prophet and the Lord.

In *Preach My Gospel*, the Lord's goals for us are clear and within the reach of us all: "Your purpose is to *invite* others to come unto Christ. . . . Go about doing good and serving people at every opportunity, whether or not they accept your message."[3] This is the counsel for missionaries and for us all. And as we each try to do our own small part to help this great work, we will discover that the act of serving others and then inviting them to come unto Christ—with both acts springing from the fountain of charity—is a very achievable goal.

---

1   2 Nephi 28:14 and Doctrine and Covenants 123:12
2   Matthew 5:16
3   *Preach My Gospel*, 11, italics added

# PART I
# ENCOURAGEMENT
# AND EXAMPLES

# PRACTICAL TRUTHS

WE CAN BECOME THE SUCCESSFUL member missionaries we wish we could be. Ironically, the keys to that success will probably come from doing less, not more, when we are asked direct questions about our faith. If that sounds strange (or wrong), hang with me. It will all make sense soon. But first, we need to remind ourselves of a few practical truths we too easily forget.

## PRACTICAL TRUTH #1: MANY PEOPLE ARE GENUINELY CURIOUS ABOUT WHO WE ARE.

It is exciting to see the fulfillment of prophecy with our own eyes. We are living in the days when the Church is coming "forth out of obscurity."[4] No matter where you live, it's hard to miss the Church. When you consider our rapidly growing membership, our temples that now dot the earth, the vastly increased numbers of full-time missionaries, the growing number of notable and famous members, the now-common Mormon "Helping Hands" T-shirts, the increasing levels of responsible news coverage from media outlets worldwide, and the remarkable effectiveness of the Church's own media efforts, the Church's profile in the world has never been greater or more accurate.

As a result, people of goodwill—which includes most people—are curious to learn more about what always seemed to be a distant religion but is now on their doorstep. Their curiosity doesn't necessarily mean that they want to join us—though some will—but their interest is genuine, and it is our privilege to answer their honest questions.

---

4  Doctrine and Covenants 1:30

## PRACTICAL TRUTH #2: MOST PEOPLE ALREADY KNOW A LOT ABOUT US, AND WHAT THEY KNOW IS GOOD.

While there is still plenty of misinformation about the Church out there, the reality is that many people understand a great deal about the Church, and what they know that is *true* is also *good*. Consider the positive things we are known for:

- We are devoted to our families.
- We live clean lives.
- We believe in helping others.
- We enjoy learning about our ancestors.
- We are honest and hardworking people.

We need never be ashamed or defensive about our membership in The Church of Jesus Christ of Latter-day Saints. The inherent goodness for which the Church is known precedes us wherever we go.

## PRACTICAL TRUTH #3: MANY PEOPLE ARE AFRAID TO ASK US ABOUT THE CHURCH.

Seems counterintuitive, doesn't it? Many people are afraid to ask about the Church, and we're afraid they might actually do it.

As I've talked with recent converts, I've found many who said they wanted to learn about the Church but were reluctant to reach out to Church members because they were afraid:

- Afraid they would give offense by accidentally saying the wrong thing.
- Afraid they would immediately have missionaries beating their door down and aggressively trying to convert them.
- Afraid of the ramifications in their own church if it was discovered they were "talking with the Mormons."
- Afraid they would face the need to change their lives.

Regardless of their reasons, their actions are the same. Many are afraid to discuss the Church, despite both their curiosity about it and their access to members who would be glad to answer their questions.

## PRACTICAL TRUTH #4: NO ONE IS AFRAID TO WATCH US.

Regardless of whether others are afraid to ask us about the Church, no one is afraid to watch us. As the Savior said, "A city that is set on a hill *cannot* be hid."[5] People know the inherent goodness of the Church and

---

5    Matthew 5:14, italics added

see confirmation of that goodness in us. In this way, the distant philosophies of "that Utah church" merge with the practical reality of our lives.

As a result, many good people are drawn to the light of the city on the hill. A portion of that light resides in each of us. And as people are attracted to the light of the gospel, questions are asked and conversations begin. Which brings us to the topic at hand—when questions come, *how do we answer them?*

## ANSWERING QUESTIONS AS THE SAVIOR DID

As in all things, we can look to the Savior for the perfect example of how to respond to the questions of others.[6] For the next few pages, we'll look at the actual ways Jesus chose to answer questions, and we'll discover why His methods were so effective.

Throughout the scriptures Jesus was constantly asked questions about His doctrine, power, and purpose. Naturally, if He chose to, He could instantly answer every question in full detail with personal experiences and supporting scriptures. *And yet He almost never did.* As we learn how Jesus answered questions, we can find the perfect models for how to effectively respond when *we* are asked to explain our faith.

### JESUS OFTEN ANSWERED QUESTIONS WITH QUESTIONS

In Luke we learn of the lawyer who attempted to trick the Savior with a question:

> And, behold, a certain lawyer stood up, and tempted him, saying, Master, what shall I do to inherit eternal life?
>
> He said unto him, What is written in the law? how readest thou?[7]

---

6   Some of the concepts discussed in these pages are adapted from the teaching guidelines developed in the *Come, Follow Me* curriculum currently being used to teach the youth of the Church. This landmark approach models itself on the teaching methods used by the Savior. It has revolutionized teaching in the Church and is revolutionizing the youth of the Church. In the years to come, the fruits of this program will be profound. Our youth will enter adulthood with stronger testimonies and a greater power to express their testimonies. They will be confident teachers in their own right at a young age. While the purpose of *Come, Follow Me* is not solely to prepare youth for more effective missionary service, that is exactly what it is doing. And because the principles are based on the actions and teaching approaches of the Savior, the same ideas will help us as we struggle and yearn to live up to the real-life challenges of hastening the work.

7   Luke 10:25–26

Obviously, if He had wanted to, the Savior could have instantly answered the lawyer's question about how to obtain eternal life. *Why didn't He?*

Responding to a question with a question is a great idea for a simple reason: It helps us understand *why* the question is being asked. Is the questioner sincere in his desire to learn? Or is he simply trying to provoke an argument?

You will answer a sincere question much differently than a question that is asked purely to provoke an argument.

By answering the lawyer's question with a question of His own—two questions actually—the Savior effortlessly probes the lawyer's scriptural *knowledge* and *understanding* before giving His answer. The Master Teacher is giving us a master class in the art of teaching.

We'll come back to our lawyer in a moment. But now, the next point to consider.

## JESUS'S FIRST ANSWERS WERE USUALLY SHORT

Nephi reminds us of the importance of the short answer. It's how we learn. "For behold, thus saith the Lord God: I will give unto the children of men line upon line, precept upon precept, here a little and there a little" (2 Nephi 28:30).

Long, windy answers rarely produce the results we seek. I know this from personal experience.

Years ago I was a new member of the Church and was studying hard to catch up in my knowledge of the gospel. An acquaintance who was not a member asked me, "So, do you really pay 10 percent of what you make to the Church? Isn't that, like, a lot of money?"

With newfound gospel knowledge almost oozing from my pores, I proceeded to explain the principle of tithing and how the money is spent, and then—since I mentioned temples in my list of tithing-supported expenses—I easily transitioned into the doctrine of temple worship, which lead to the power and authority of the priesthood, which led me back to Joseph Smith, which lead me to the origins of the Book of Mormon, which led me (rather neatly, I thought) to Moroni's promise.

All of this took about ten to fifteen minutes. When I finally stopped talking, I was proud of myself for having worked in most of at least two missionary discussions while challenging my friend to dig deeper and learn more.

But my friend showed a different response. His eyes were glazed over, and he had the look of someone caught in a rainstorm without an umbrella. I realized that for most of my lecture he had simply been waiting out of politeness for me to stop talking. He was also, I'm pretty sure, sorry he'd asked in the first place.

The way doctrines fit together in the gospel is a beautiful thing, and one doctrine really does lead to another. But when people come to us for a quick cup of water, it does no one any good to turn a fire hose on them.

Line upon line. Here a little, there a little. Keep it simple. Keep it short.

To my friend who asked if I paid tithing, all I needed to say was, "Well, yes, I do. I thought it would be hard, but it really hasn't been difficult." And then I should have *stopped talking.*

When we give long, run-on answers to questions, we presume to know where the questioner wants to go with the conversation, which is both arrogant and rude. A short answer knocks the ball cleanly back to his side of the court. Then it's his choice. If he wants to know more, he'll ask, and you'll know how to precisely help *him* instead of just throwing a lot of doctrine against a wall to see what sticks.

If your brief answer satisfies his interest, he'll say thanks and move on, but he'll know that you are someone who can answer questions about the Church without burying him in a verbal avalanche—and knowing that will greatly increase the odds that at some point he'll ask you another question.

Hopefully you can get to the second question because—trust me on this—*the first question is never the real question.* It's just a test question to see how you'll respond. If your friend judges you as windy, pushy, or uncaring, you'll never hear the second question—the real one on his mind.

But if you'll pass the "test," the second question will allow you to catch a glimpse into your friend's heart and find out how you can best help him.

Want an example? Let's go back to the Savior and the lawyer. The lawyer asks, "What must I do to inherit eternal life?" The Savior, perceiving the lawyer to be a man with at least basic religious training, asks, "What do the scriptures say?"

The lawyer responds, "Thou shalt love the Lord thy God with all thy heart, and with all thy soul, and with all thy strength, and with all thy mind; and thy neighbor as thyself."

And the Savior, capable of delivering the majestic Sermon on the Mount, responds here with only a few words. "Thou hast answered right: this do, and thou shalt live" (Luke 10:27–28).

Could Jesus have been any simpler? Any kinder? Any more direct?

And, as we've learned, His short answer invites a second question, and the second question inevitably reveals the intent of the first.

"But he, willing to justify himself, said unto Jesus, And who is my neighbour?" (Luke 10:29). With this second question, the lawyer opens his soul. And Jesus—who by virtue of the lawyer's second question has been *given permission* to delve deeper into the gospel—responds with the story of the Good Samaritan, a tale so revered that the term itself is universally understood to be someone who reaches out to others in difficult circumstances with no thought of personal reward.

Behold the power of the short answer that leads to a second question.

Remember, precept on precept. Milk before meat. Keep it simple; keep it short. In later pages we'll go over how to give short, simple answers to basic questions about the Church. But for now, just understand why the short answer *works*.

## JESUS WASN'T AFRAID OF SILENCE

As the saying goes, nature abhors a vacuum. When a conversation lulls, all parties feel the need to come up with something to say. If the pause continues for more than a few seconds, the silence can become uncomfortable.

Except for the Savior. Jesus was not afraid to pause . . . to wait . . . to see what would happen next.

We've heard the story of the woman taken in adultery. Let's examine it in a new light:

> The scribes and Pharisees brought unto him a woman taken in adultery; and when they had set her in the midst,
>
> They say unto him, Master, this woman was taken in adultery, in the very act.
>
> Now Moses in the law commanded us, that such should be stoned: but what sayest thou?
>
> This they said, tempting him, that they might have to accuse him. But Jesus stooped down, and with his finger wrote on the ground, as though he heard them not.[8]

---

8   John 8:3–6

The tension in the air was probably thick enough to cut with a knife. And yet Jesus simply *stopped*. He took a time out. We don't know for how long, but at the moment it likely seemed an eternity. And then he looked up and offered the immortal words: "He that is without sin among you, let him cast the first stone at her" (John 8:7).

And then he paused *again*:

And again he stooped down, and wrote upon the ground.

And they which heard it, being convicted by their own conscience, went out one by one, beginning at the eldest, even unto the last: and Jesus was left alone, and the woman standing in the midst.[9]

It is easy to marvel at the simple beauty of Jesus's response to the woman's accusers, but let's take a moment to marvel at the beauty of those two moments of silence. Why did He do it?

A pause can accomplish a lot in a conversation:

- It gives us a moment to think, to regroup, and even to await inspiration.
- It doesn't necessarily add tension to a conversation. In fact, it can sometimes drain tension out of a situation like air out of a balloon.
- It shows respect for the questioner, as he sees you are taking his question seriously and not just spouting off glib, trite answers.
- As you pause after giving the answer, it allows you to *see what happens next*.

In the story of Jesus and the woman taken in adultery, the first pause drained the tension. The second pause allowed Him to see what would happen next. The accusers dropped their stones, one by one, and departed.

Once again, the Master displays his mastery.

## Jesus spoke to be understood

What does that mean? It means that Jesus taught people with words and images already familiar to them so they could better understand his message. Here's an example: "And great multitudes were gathered unto him, . . . And he spake many things unto them in parables, saying, Behold, a sower went forth to sow" (Matthew 13:2–3).

Beginning with that verse, the Savior gives the people the parable of the sower, explaining how seeds can only grow properly if they are cared

---

9  John 8:8–9

for correctly. He reminds us of the need to nurture our own testimony. The point: Jesus compared the gospel to things His listeners already understood. In the agrarian-based economy of the time, His audience could instantly relate to the image of a planter sowing seeds.

In the same vein, we should describe the gospel in ways that make sense today. For example, if someone asked me what it's like to receive personal revelation, I might say something like, "It's hard to explain, but it's almost as if *knowledge* is suddenly being downloaded into my brain from a celestial mainframe—and along with it, a feeling of being wrapped in pure love and understanding." Such a description would have fallen on deaf ears to the farmers, fishermen, and merchants of Jesus's time, but today it would make reasonable sense.

So when we talk to others about the gospel, we should make sure we're talking to them in their language, not ours. Many Church terms we take for granted are incomprehensible to our nonmember friends. Fortunately, it's not hard to make substitutions. Here's a partial list:

| Instead of: | Try: |
| --- | --- |
| Ward | Congregation |
| Ward building | Meeting hall; sanctuary |
| Bishop | Pastor; minister |
| Stake | Several congregations united by geography, similar to a Catholic diocese |
| Relief Society | The Church organization for women |
| Primary | The Sunday classes for children |
| Mutual | The weeknight activities for youth (teenagers) |
| Sacrament meeting | Our main Sunday worship service where we receive the sacrament and listen to sermons |
| Seminary | Morning scripture study class for teenagers |
| The Atonement | The Savior's grace |
| The Bible | The Holy Bible |

Please note that last one—the name of the Bible is not the *Bible*. It is the *Holy Bible*. (Check your scriptures if you don't believe me.) This is important. Most people know that we believe the Book of Mormon to be scripture, but sometimes people think that we put the Book of Mormon above the Holy Bible. When we refer to the Bible as the *Holy Bible*, we demonstrate our reverence for that sacred book and also bolster our claim that we are, in fact, Christian.

So, then, how can we answer questions about the gospel most effectively? By following Christ's example:

- He often answered questions with questions of his own.
- His first answers were usually short.
- He was not afraid to pause.
- He used language and images his listeners would understand.

With these proven principles in mind, we can now tackle the questions most likely to be asked by people who are curious about our faith. In these pages we'll assume that the person asking is doing so in a spirit of friendship and honest inquiry. When that's the case, it's our privilege to answer their questions briefly and succinctly.

But sometimes it's not that easy, and there may be times when we need to delay giving them an answer. Or there may be times when we will choose *not* to answer a question. We'll look at how to deal with those sometimes tense situations at the end of the book. But for now, don't worry. These pages should fill the need 90 percent of the time.

# PART 2
## GOOD ANSWERS
## TO GOOD QUESTIONS

IN THE PAGES THAT FOLLOW, you'll see questions and ideas for short answers. As you read the answers, your mind may begin to launch in a million directions with things you'll want to add, but remember, your short answer is intended to be *short*. As you read these answers, envision yourself saying something equally brief, and then *stop talking*! Act as the Savior did: speak briefly, pause, and see what happens next.

And just like the Savior did, remember that it's always okay to begin with a question of your own to help determine the point of view your friend is bringing to the discussion. (You don't *have* to begin with a question, but it's always an option.) For example, "That's a good question. Is there a particular reason you're asking?" Or, "Well, what have *you* heard about _____ (polygamy, temple worship, etc.)?"

Along with the short answers that follow, you'll find some accompanying thoughts that may help to enhance your own background and perspective on the subject. And there is always a scripture or two for support.

A word of advice: don't overlook the scriptures! It's true that some who come to us will have no church background. But many others will be Christians who belong to other churches. Many will know the scriptures well. So should we.

While living in the South, I learned that Bible study is a way of life there. I've known investigators who were sincerely interested in the gospel but came away frustrated because the missionaries couldn't adequately back up their claims with scriptures. Instead, the stymied missionaries would simply bear their testimony and move on to the next subject. But to scripture-loving investigators, a testimony that doesn't appear to be based on scriptural principles is not likely to kindle a fire in their hearts.

We should recognize this and be careful not to hide behind our testimonies. In the end, our friends and investigators will see testimonies as feelings, and while feelings are good, facts are fundamental. As our conversation deepens, we must be able to defend what we say. In a best-case scenario, it goes like this:

- You present the gospel principle or doctrine.
- You support it with a scripture.
- You share how living the principle has blessed your life.
- You bear testimony of the truthfulness of the principle.

This isn't to overwhelm you. You won't need all of this for your short first response—and your short first response is what this book is about. But you may need it for your second. And you'll almost certainly need it for your third. You don't have to become a dusty scriptorian, ready to elaborate on the family lines of the kings of the Northern Kingdom,[10] but you should be able to find basic scriptures to support the principles of tithing, baptism for the dead, the three degrees of glory, the apostasy, etc.

Of course, you'll find the basic ones here.

By referring back to the scriptures listed in this book or by creating a quick reference guide of your own favorites, you (1) won't have to memorize them all but (2) in the process find that you've memorized some of them anyway. As my children and grandchildren say, it's all good.

One more quick point. As you read through these responses, you'll see that sometimes an idea or phrase used in one response turns up in another. Sometimes there are basic points concerning doctrine that need to be made in more than one situation. You'll see how this works right from the start.

Let's begin.

---

10 Although, if you're interested, you'll find it all in 1 Kings and 2 Kings. Enjoy your reading.

# QUESTIONS ABOUT OUR CHRISTIANITY AND GOD'S GRACE

### Question #1: Are you Christian?

**The short answer:** "Yes, absolutely. I believe in God the Father, in His Son, Jesus Christ, and in the Holy Ghost. I believe that Jesus is my personal Savior as well as the Savior of the whole earth and that it is *only* through His grace that we are able to return to live with Him in heaven."

The essential points you will want to make are
1. You believe in the Holy Trinity (we call it the Godhead).
2. You have accepted Jesus Christ as your personal Savior.
3. You recognize Christ as the Savior of all mankind.
4. You fully understand that it is only through the grace (Atonement) of Jesus Christ that we are able to progress in the next life.

Anything less than these four points will leave you vulnerable to criticism that Latter-day Saints are not Christian. But the good news is that all four of these doctrines are fully embraced by the Church.

## SCRIPTURE SUPPORT:

Usually we will want to demonstrate our support of gospel truths with scriptures from the Holy Bible, but in this case our best support comes from latter-day scriptures as we make our case for our basic Christianity and that the Book of Mormon is truly a second witness of Jesus Christ.

| 2 Nephi 25:26 | We talk of Christ, we rejoice in Christ, we preach of Christ . . . |
| Moroni 10:32 | Yea, come unto Christ . . . then is his grace sufficient for you . . . |
| 2 Nephi 33:6 | I glory in my Jesus, for he hath redeemed my soul from hell |
| Doctrine and Covenants 76:22 | This is the testimony . . . that we give of him: That he lives! |

Your friend could follow up with any number of questions—depending on what he knows (or thinks he knows) about the Church. For example, if you share Book of Mormon scriptures with him, he may ask about the Book of Mormon and its origin. If his goal is to argue, he will likely respond to your short answer by "telling you what you really believe." If so, don't argue. See the section on ending arguments in the last part of the book.

### Question #2: Is the Mormon Church a cult?

This is a loaded question because the word is (1) emotionally charged and (2) very difficult to define in normal conversation. If you ask fifty people to tell you what a cult is, you will likely hear fifty different answers. Even if the question is asked with goodwill, if you respond by using the word *cult* in your answer (as in, "No, we are not a cult"), you will end up trying to justify yourself by satisfying someone else's unique definition of a nebulous and negative word. It is a no-win situation that will accomplish nothing. The best approach is to change the premise of the question with your answer.

> **The short answer:** "Actually, we are a Christian church. We believe in God the Father and His Son, Jesus Christ, and in the Holy Ghost. I believe that Jesus is my personal Savior as well as the Savior of the whole earth and that it is *only* through His grace that we are able to return to live with Him in heaven."

## SCRIPTURE SUPPORT:

Your goal (as in Question #1) is to clearly state your claim for being Christian. Therefore, your support scriptures are the same as those in Question #1:

| | |
|---|---|
| 2 Nephi 25:26 | We talk of Christ, we rejoice in Christ, we preach of Christ . . . |
| Moroni 10:32 | Yea, come unto Christ . . . then is his grace sufficient for you . . . |
| 2 Nephi 33:6 | I glory in my Jesus, for he hath redeemed my soul from hell |
| Doctrine and Covenants 76:22 | This is the testimony . . . that we give of him: That he lives! |

## OTHER SUPPORT:

See Mormon.org for another thoughtful response to "Why do some call Mormonism a cult?" You'll find it under FAQ at www.mormon.org.

Asking if the LDS Church is a cult is simply another way of asking if the Church is Christian—the question is just coming from a more negative viewpoint. After hearing your short answer, your friend will have to put his cards on the table and ask about specific concerns he may have about the Church. To the extent you can answer his honest questions, do. To the extent that you choose to delay your answer or choose to not continue the conversation, see part 3 of this book—*A Time to Speak, a Time to Keep Silence*—for direction on ending arguments.

### Question #3: *What makes your church different?*

As it turns out, I've been asked this question more often than any other. It is, of course, completely open-ended. The problem is that open-ended questions can lead us into some very long and windy answers, which will likely not be a blessing to the one on the receiving end of our rambling discourse.

But here's an idea: When I'm asked this question, I change it. After all, as we attempt to convince the world that we are, in fact, Christians, why answer this question by immediately talking about our differences? Why not talk about our similarities—which your friend will probably find equally interesting and possibly surprising.

> **The short answer:** "Well, first of all, even though we do have some differences, we have *way* more things in common than you might guess. We believe in God the Father and His Son, Jesus Christ, and in the Holy Ghost. I believe that Jesus is my personal Savior as well as the Savior of the whole earth and that it is *only* through His grace that we are able to return to live with Him in heaven.
>
> "But we do have some differences. One of them is the Book of Mormon. It's a book that we believe to be additional scripture that testifies, just like the Holy Bible, that Jesus is the Christ. Have you ever heard of the Book of Mormon?"

Okay, that's a little longer, but you can see the direction. First, quickly emphasize what we have in common. Then mention a single difference (such as the Book of Mormon, the Restoration, temples, living prophets, continuing revelation, etc.) and see where the conversation goes. Prime it by asking a question of your own, as in the example above.

### SUPPORT SCRIPTURES:

For our commonality with other Christians, see the scripture support list for Question #1. To support the Book of Mormon with references from the Holy Bible see

| | |
|---|---|
| Ezekiel 37:16 | The stick of Joseph, the stick of Judah |
| John 10:16 | And other sheep I have, which are not of this fold |

## *Question #4: What do you believe about Jesus?*

One of the criticisms of the Church is that, "Well, they say they believe in Jesus, but it's not the Jesus that I know," and then they focus on perceived differences between how Latter-day Saints understand Christ versus a more traditional Protestant view of Him.

While we do have some doctrinal differences with mainline Christian churches (for example, we believe that Christ is our literal elder brother, separate from the Father, and possesses a tangible body), there is much more that unites us with other churches than divides us. It is not dishonest to stress our commonality rather than our differences. We don't hide our differences, but we don't need to beat people over the head with them.

> **The short answer**: "We believe that Jesus Christ is the Savior of the world and is the Son of God the Father. We believe that Christ came to earth to pay the price for our sins. We believe that while He was on the earth, He organized His church, was crucified, and arose on the third day. We believe He lives today, that He has restored His Church, and that one day He will return in power and glory to the earth."

**The point:** Even as we are emphasizing how we agree on the Savior and His role in the salvation of the human race, we are still planting seeds—that He organized a specific church and restored it in the latter days and that He will return again to claim His Church and people.

## SCRIPTURE SUPPORT:

| | |
|---|---|
| Isaiah 53:4 | Surely he hath borne our griefs . . . he was wounded for our transgressions |
| Matthew 16:15–19 | Jesus: Whom say ye that I am? Peter: Thou art the Christ |
| John 14:6 | I am the way, the truth, and the life |
| John 3:16 | For God so loved the world, that he gave his only begotten Son |
| Acts 1:11 | This same Jesus . . . shall come (again) in like manner as ye have seen |

### *Question #5: Do you believe that God and Jesus are separate beings?*

This is a straightforward question that should be answered directly. We state our beliefs simply, concisely, and without embellishment.

> **The short answer:** "We believe that God the Father, His Son, Jesus Christ, and the Holy Ghost are all separate beings though they are united in one purpose. We also believe that God the Father and Jesus Christ exist within tangible and glorified bodies."

This goes against the "God the Cloud" concept prevalent in much of modern Christianity. The idea that the Trinity (Godhead) is all one and yet simultaneously separate is simply presented as "a mystery." It is born from scriptures such as John 4:24, "God is a Spirit; and they that worship him must worship in spirit and in truth."

This is a time when we must accept that people of goodwill can, and often will, interpret the things of God differently than we do. But we can certainly defend our position.

## SCRIPTURE SUPPORT:

| | |
|---|---|
| Matthew 3:16–17 | Jesus baptized, the Holy Ghost descends as a dove, the Father's voice approves (three separate beings simultaneously present) |
| Luke 24:39 | A spirit hath not flesh and bones as ye see I have (spoken by Jesus following His Resurrection) |
| Exodus 31:18 | The Ten Commandments written by the finger of God |
| Acts 7:56 | Stephen sees Jesus standing on the right hand of the Father |
| Joseph Smith—History 1:17 | "When the light rested upon me I saw two Personages . . . standing above me in the air" |

## Question #6: If you're Christian, why don't you have crosses in your churches?

The reality is that this issue is a major sticking point for many people who struggle to accept our claim of Christianity. The Star of David for Judaism, the crescent moon for Islam, the yin and yang for Taoism, the cross for Christianity—all are symbols universally recognized and understood.

Then here come the Latter-day Saints.

Members of the Church will likely be explaining our answer to this question until the Second Coming. Here is one that might work for you.

> **The short answer:** "We never want to offend anyone, but we believe that displaying the cross tends to draw undue attention to Christ's mortal suffering. Instead of focusing on His death, we focus on the living Christ and His victory over pain and sin. And in any case, we feel that our discipleship isn't measured by outward signs but by our inner commitment to love Him and follow His commandments."

## SCRIPTURE SUPPORT:

Luke 24:5          Why seek ye the living among the dead?

## ADDITIONAL SUPPORT:

"Q&A: Why don't we use crosses in our churches?" *New Era*, September 1996.

Some will point out that Paul frequently used the term *cross* as a metaphor for trials to be overcome by Christ's grace (Atonement)[11] and that during His life, even Christ used the word as a metaphor for life's challenges.[12] This, they will argue, shows that the cross was

---

11   Paul uses this image repeatedly. See, for example, Galatians 6:14 and 1 Corinthians 1:18.

12   For example, Luke 9:23, "And he said to them all, If any man will come after me, let him deny himself, and take up his cross daily, and follow me." In modern revelation, Christ continues to employ the term as in Doctrine and Covenants 56:2, "And he that will not take up his cross and follow me, and keep my commandments, the same shall not be saved."

always understood to be a symbol of Christ and His teaching, and we (Mormons) are therefore in error in discarding an image that even Christ Himself endorsed. You might choose to counter this with the idea that the cross was only one of *many* images that have endured through the centuries as symbols of Christ and which He sometimes used in describing himself. Among others are the Dove, Lamb, Lawgiver, Manna, Living Water, Rock, and the bread/wine/water of the sacrament—any of which could represent the mission of Christ with no loss of poetic and inspirational power.[13]

We should recognize, though, that some will not accept this or any other explanation for our no-cross policy, and they may even call our claim of Christianity into question over this issue. In this case we may need to simply state our case with courtesy and compassion and agree to disagree.[14]

---

13   See the Topical Guide: "Jesus Christ, Types of, In Anticipation" for a list of scriptural symbols of Christ throughout the ages.

14   See Jeffrey R. Holland, "The Costs—and Blessings—of Discipleship," general conference, April 2014.

### Question #7: Is it true that you don't believe in God's grace but think you can "work" your way to heaven?

One of the favorite complaints of those who oppose the Church is that we believe that our ability to progress in the Eternal world is based solely and completely on our works in life and put little or no stock in the traditional Christian view of the grace of Jesus Christ. They can point to any number of general conference addresses (especially older ones) that remind us that we risk our chance for eternal progression whenever we fall short of obeying God's commandments.[15] Elder Gene R. Cook acknowledged as much in the April 1993 conference, when he felt the need to devote his entire talk to explaining that the Church does, in fact, believe in God's grace. But he acknowledged that many members didn't fully understand this basic doctrine. Speaking of Church members in general, he said, "Some of us [don't know] how to use the great gift of grace the Father has given to us through the Atonement of His Son Jesus Christ."[16]

I believe it's true that we *do* put more focus on bringing our actions in line with our beliefs than many churches, but that doesn't mean we overlook or trivialize Christ's power to literally save us—and that His power is the *only* way our salvation can be achieved. This doctrine is taught not only in the Holy Bible but with equal strength in the Book of Mormon and Doctrine and Covenants, as you'll see in the list below.

So when you are asked the question, here is a straightforward and brief answer:

**The short answer:** "I'm glad you asked. No, that's not true. Like all Christians, we believe in doing our best to keep God's

---

15  See, for example, N. Eldon Tanner, "Obedience," general conference, October 1973. Near the end of his talk he says, "Only as we live and keep the commandments of God, being obedient in all things can we fully enjoy life here and eternal life in the world to come." Nowhere in the talk does President Tanner mention the Atonement, the eventual need we will all have for repentance, or the fact that perfect obedience is not possible in life. Instead, his use of the term only suggests that our eternal progression hinges solely on our works. I'm confident President Tanner didn't believe this to be literally true, but his remarks, I believe, were in keeping with the general Church culture and tone of the time.

16  See Gene R. Cook, "Receiving Divine Assistance through the Grace of the Lord," general conference, April 1993.

commandments, but we agree with Paul that 'all have sinned and come short of the glory of God' and that only through the grace of Jesus Christ can we be saved from our sins."

## SCRIPTURE SUPPORT:

| | |
|---|---|
| Romans 3:23 | All have sinned and come short of the glory of God |
| Ephesians 2:8–9 | By grace are ye saved, not by works, lest any man should boast |
| Moroni 10:32 | By his grace ye may be perfect in Christ |
| Doctrine and Covenants 17:8 | My grace is sufficient . . . and you shall be lifted up at the last day |

If a conversation develops on this subject, it will likely morph into the centuries-old question of faith versus works; or, in other words, to what extent do our works qualify us as better disciples of Christ? Do we earn a higher reward in the eternities because of our works?

Here is a very short summary of our basic position, which may be useful.

The Holy Bible itself offers doctrine on this subject that could be interpreted as contradictory. Compare Ephesians 2:8–9 to James 2:20, 24 (20–26), for a classic example of dueling scriptures:

> For by grace are ye saved through faith; and that not of yourselves: it is the gift of God:
> Not of works, lest any man should boast. (Ephesians 2:8–9)

Versus

> But wilt thou know, O vain man, that faith without works is dead?
> . . . by works a man is justified, and not by faith only. (James 2:20, 24)

How do you reconcile these two scriptures? Can it be done?

It can. Here's one example of how. In Luke 10 you find two stories placed back to back. The first is the story we've already visited—the lawyer who asks the Savior, "Who is my neighbor?" and receives in response the story of the Good Samaritan (see Luke 10:25–37).

But the story of the Good Samaritan is immediately followed with the story of Mary and Martha in which the Savior reminds the overworked-by-choice Martha that she needs to slow down and smell the gospel roses (Luke 10:38–42).

Two stories, side by side, seemingly unrelated. But are they?

In the first story, the lawyer essentially asks, "What is the smallest number of people I can love and still be accepted in Your sight?" Jesus responds that he must love everyone, even people previously considered enemies.[17]

In the second story, Mary sits at the feet of the Savior while Martha serves the guests. Martha becomes angry and wants Mary to help. Jesus tells Martha she needs to put down her work and recognize that her best choice right now is not to serve food and drink, but to receive manna and living water from the Savior himself.

How do these back-to-back stories fit together? Both tackle the problem of faith versus works but from opposite directions. The lawyer is in danger of missing the gospel because he is doing too little. His lack of works—reaching out to others in need—is stunting his spiritual growth. Martha is in danger of missing the gospel because she is doing too much. Her compulsion to work—even when the Savior is present—is stunting her spiritual growth.

Here, then, is the answer to the question you can share with your friend. We need to strike a middle ground. In the scriptures, some needed to be taught to reach for the spiritual strength that comes from serving others, *and so they received instruction tailored to fit their specific needs.* Others needed to be challenged to slow down and rely more on faith, and so they received instruction tailored to fit *their* specific needs.

The twin concepts of faith and works are not at war. Rather, they support each other beautifully. But we Latter-day Saints, who frequently worry that we aren't doing enough, need to remember (with our sister Martha) that our works are a barometer of our faith, not a recipe for our salvation.[18]

---

17   There was great friction and animosity between the Jews and the Samaritans, and both sides went to lengths to avoid the other. See, for example, John 4:9 and Matthew 10:5.

18   For my money, the two best explanations of the role of faith vs. works can be found in Brad Wilcox, "His Grace Is Sufficient," *Ensign*, September 2013, and Stephen Robinson, *Believing Christ: The Parable of the Bicycle and Other Good News*, Deseret Book Co., 1992.

**Question #8: Why do Mormons claim they are the only ones who can be touched by the Spirit (Holy Ghost)?**

Other than the Atonement, the "unspeakable gift of the Holy Ghost" (Doctrine and Covenants 121:26) may be the Lord's greatest gift to us in mortality. Part of that gift is what we call the Light of Christ[19] (sometimes described as our conscience) that helps us to know, without knowing how we know, what is right and wrong. For believers of Christ in all churches, the Holy Ghost blesses the faithful with inspiration and knowledge beyond mortal understanding. The gift of conscience and inspiration are two examples of how the Holy Ghost can bless all humanity, not just those who are members of The Church of Jesus Christ of Latter-day Saints.

I have had the opportunity to listen to other Christians who are not LDS bear powerful testimony of the reality of Holy Ghost and its direct impact on their lives. Many of us who are converts can remember sacred experiences prior to joining the Church when we have felt the Spirit's influence. It is a humbling and beautiful reminder that God is truly no respecter of persons (see Acts 10:34).

Yet we believe, and our missionaries teach, that only in The Church of Jesus Christ of Latter-day Saints can we receive the right to the constant companionship of the Holy Ghost by the laying on of hands by one who holds the authority. This is a serious problem for our friends from other Christian churches. Many devout Christians, who have experienced many tender mercies from the Holy Ghost, consider our statement to be ignorant, arrogant, and disrespectful. A few have told me so while sitting in my living room.

We need to tread carefully here, or we will seem to trivialize the sacred experiences of others—the very thing that we resent so deeply when it happens to us.

> **The short answer:** "I don't have to tell you about the power and beauty of the Holy Ghost. Just like you, I know it is tangible proof that my Father in Heaven knows and loves me personally. And in our Church, by the power and authority of

---

19   See Moroni 7:19; also Dallin H. Oaks, "Always Have His Spirit," general conference, October 1996—one of several talks that discuss the Light of Christ as a gift given freely to all mankind regardless of their belief in Jesus Christ.

the priesthood, we are given the right to receive an even greater measure of the Holy Spirit than is commonly experienced in the world."

**The point:** We must be careful to let our Christian friend know that we are not belittling his own experiences with the Holy Ghost but sharing with him the news that in the Church he can feel the Spirit in richer abundance. Nevertheless, I have seen even this statement received with heavy skepticism. The good news is that if you are a convert to the Church, you will be able to share your own experience and testify to the truthfulness of this doctrine. But if you are not a convert from another Christian church—then *go back to your ward or stake and talk to someone who is.* You will need to be able to relate the firsthand story of yourself or another Church member on this point. If your inquiring friend is truly bothered by this claim and you can't share a first-person experience about it, then offer to have him meet with your fellow ward member (with the member's permission of course).

In addition to your own testimony, you may also wish to share this story told by Dallin H. Oaks:

> A newly baptized member told me what she felt when she received that gift. This was a faithful Christian woman who had spent her life in service to others. She knew and loved the Lord, and had felt the manifestations of His Spirit. When she received the added light of the restored gospel, she was baptized and the elders placed their hands upon her head and gave her the gift of the Holy Ghost. She recalled, "I felt the influence of the Holy Ghost settle upon me with greater intensity than I had ever felt before. He was like an old friend who had guided me in the past, but now had come to stay.[20]

Church members and missionaries are often caught by surprise from the amount of blowback we receive for this doctrine. Let's not be caught by surprise but be ready to defend our doctrine and our faith while respecting the sacred experiences of others.

---

20    From Dallin H. Oaks, "Always Have His Spirit," general conference, October 1996.

## SCRIPTURE SUPPORT:

Acts 8:14–20                          Peter and John bestow the Holy
                                      Ghost by the laying on of hands.
                                      Simon offers them money to give
                                      him that authority

Doctrine and Covenants 20:43          Duties of elders: to confirm the
                                      church by the laying on of hands,
                                      and the giving of the Holy Ghost

### Question #9: Why do you say that you "know" the gospel is true? Don't you really just believe it?

Just as the preceding question on the Holy Ghost will most likely come from someone with a deeper understanding of the scriptures, this question will most likely come from someone without a scriptural or religious background. To the unbeliever or skeptic, the idea that you can "know" anything pertaining to God is illogical at best, an exercise in self-delusion at worst. They will concede that you *have faith* in something or *believe* it to be true (most likely, in their view, in the absence of hard evidence), but the idea that you *know* that God lives in the same way you know the sun will come up tomorrow morning may be greeted by some with dismissal or scorn.

Nevertheless, if you are asked the question, it is your privilege to respond. If your testimony is met with disbelief, you can take heart in these words from Elder Holland:

> To [you], I say, dear child, you have in your own humble way stepped into a circle of very distinguished women and men who have, as the Book of Mormon prophet Jacob said, "view[ed Christ's] death, and suffer[ed] his cross and [borne] the shame of the world."[21]

So if the question comes, explain with all the courage and courtesy you can muster[22] how you (and we and he) can know the truths of the gospel for ourselves.

**The short answer:** "I admit that sounds like a bold statement. I can only say that I have prayed to God to know if He lives and if the gospel is true, and in response He filled both my mind and heart with a burst of knowledge unlike anything I have ever experienced before. And He continues to bless me from time to time with this kind of knowledge. To say anything less than 'I know that God lives' would be to dishonor Him and the sacred experiences I have shared with Him and continue to share with Him. And there are millions of others who have

---

21   See Jacob 1:8, and Jeffrey R. Holland, "The Cost—and Blessings—of Discipleship," general conference, April 2014. Brackets in quoted material preserved from referenced source.

22   Ibid., Holland

had the same experience. Could I share a scripture verse with you that helped me understand how this works?"

**The point:** We covered a lot of ground in that short answer.

- Acknowledge it is difficult to understand if it hasn't happened to you.
- Explain in as few words as possible what it's like to receive "the burning in the bosom"[23] that the Holy Ghost brings.
- Explain that this was not a one-time experience but that the Holy Ghost continues to bless your life with pure knowledge.
- Let your friend know that these experiences are sacred.
- Testify that millions of others have had the same experience.
- Offer to share Moroni's promise (Moroni 10:3–5).

To the skeptic, there is no point in sharing scripture stories where revelation is given and received. If he doesn't accept the scriptures, he won't accept your stories. The best you can do is share Moroni 10:3–5 and invite him to put Moroni's challenge to the test. He may accept the challenge, or he may not. Or he may finally accept it twenty years later.

One final thought—there is another type of person who may ask the question of how you can *know* the things of God: the individual without religious background but who is nevertheless looking for truth in his life. To this person, the idea that spiritual truths can be known may be a new and strange concept. "Who am I," he might think, "to be able to know the truth of God when so many great minds through the centuries have tried and only come to confusion?"

If you encounter any of us out there—and I say "us" because my wife and I were both in that group before we met, married, and joined the Church—then you hold a precious soul in your hands. Share Moroni's promise, and tell them that there *is* a central truth and it *can* be known. Then invite them not to take your word for it but to find out for themselves. Plant the seed carefully, love them for their seeking hearts, and then trust the harvest to the Lord.

**SCRIPTURE SUPPORT:**

| | |
|---|---|
| Moroni 10:3–5 | When you receive these things, ask God, in the name of Christ, if these things are not true |

---

23   Doctrine and Covenants 9:8, "I will cause that your bosom to burn within you."

Joseph Smith—History 1:25      I knew it, and I knew that God knew it, and I could not deny it

Doctrine and Covenants 76:22      This is the testimony . . . which we give of him: That he lives!

### Question #10: Do you believe that you're all going to become gods?

President Lorenzo Snow's famous couplet, "As man is, God once was; as God is, man may become,"[24] has long inspired believers and troubled critics. The question of whether Mormons believe we're going to become gods is not a question likely to come up in casual conversation. Usually it will come from someone who has been exposed to anti-Mormon literature. He may or may not consider himself to be anti-Mormon. If he is, he is probably just looking for something to argue about. But he may be honestly seeking your viewpoint on what—to his mind—is an unusual doctrine. This is a very good time to respond to a question with a question: "It's an interesting subject. Why do you ask?"

Either way, this is not a question that lends itself to a short answer.

**The short answer:** "That's a question that would take longer to answer than we have time for now. But in general, we believe that God the Father is literally the Father of our spirits and that He loves us like an actual father. Like any father He wants us to grow and develop and someday inherit what He now possesses. There are several scriptures from the Holy Bible that support this idea. If you're really interested, could we set a time to talk about it later?"

### SCRIPTURE SUPPORT:

| | |
|---|---|
| Philippians 2:5–6 | Be of the same mind as Jesus, who thought it not robbery to be equal with God |
| Romans 8:16–17 | We are children of God, and if children, then heirs, heirs of God |
| 2 Peter 1:4 | Great and precious promises to be partakers of the divine nature |
| John 10:33–34 | Is it not written in your law that ye are gods? |
| Revelation 3:21 | He who overcomes will sit with me on my throne |

---

24  Quoted by Spencer W. Kimball, "Our Great Potential," general conference, April 1977.

Doctrine and Covenants 88:7     Exalted saints will be made equal
                                to the Father
Doctrine and Covenants 132:20   Then they shall be gods, because
                                they have no end

**ADDITIONAL SUPPORT:**

If your friend is genuinely interested in this topic, you will likely
want to refresh your mind on the subject. You can find an excellent
article at lds.org under Gospel Topics—Becoming Like God. It's a
long article, but it explains and defends the doctrine with accuracy and
historical context.

Also, see President Kimball's April 1977 general conference address,
"Our Great Potential," that discusses the doctrine in a straightforward
way.

### Question #11: Are you saved?

I'm convinced that sometimes people ask us if we believe we are saved only to watch us stumble all over ourselves.

Ask a Mormon if he is saved, and you are likely to get a long, rambling answer as he tries to sort through the three degrees of glory, explain the characteristics of each, and explain that while all of them are far better than this life—bathed as they are in great light, knowledge, and glory—it is the celestial kingdom he seeks, and it is not certain yet that he will obtain it, but he hopes to, and if it's a lesser kingdom, he's not really sure if he'll be happy about it or not.

If you ask a fellow Christian of another faith if he is saved, he will say, "Yes."

We need not worry about answering the question of whether or not we are saved. The traditional and general definition of the word *saved* is one who has accepted Jesus Christ as his personal Savior, has felt the Holy Spirit in his life confirming the power of Christ to bring about his salvation, and who therefore has a bright and lively hope (see 1 Peter 1:3) of his eventual resurrection into a kingdom of glory beyond anything he can now comprehend.

All of which sounds like good Mormon doctrine to me.

> **The short answer:** "Yes, and isn't it wonderful? I have accepted Jesus Christ as my personal Savior and am doing my best to live by His teachings. And when I fall short, I know that His grace will keep me from being cast off."

There are, of course, nuances to this doctrine and biblical scriptures that emphatically teach that becoming "saved" must be more than a one-time experience in the life of a Christian. Consider Peter's condemnation of the backsliding believer:

> For if after they have escaped the pollutions of the world through the knowledge of the Lord and Saviour Jesus Christ, they are again entangled therein, and overcome, the latter end is worse with them than the beginning.
>
> For it had been better for them not to have known the way of righteousness, than, after they have known it, to turn from the holy commandment delivered unto them.[25]

---

25   2 Peter 2:20–21

Or consider the testimony of James, known by all Mormons, that we read earlier: "But wilt thou know, O vain man, that faith without works is dead? . . . By works a man is justified, and not by faith only" (James 2:20, 24).

These scriptures make it clear that the Lord expects us to *live* the gospel and not just accept it. This brings us back to the faith versus works debate explored in Question #7, but we must remember that since all have sinned and fall short of the glory of God (see Romans 3:23), our capacity to earn anything is extremely limited, and it is only the grace (Atonement) of Christ that enables us to progress eternally.

So after confidently sharing the good news that through the grace of Christ you are saved, consider asking a question of your friend: "But now I'm interested in your opinion on a question I've often thought about. Let's say someone is saved in his youth, but in his later years he seems to turn away from his Christian roots. He becomes a drunkard and commits crimes and mocks the things of God. If he dies in this state, does he still enjoy the same degree of salvation as the believer who has spent his life following the Savior to the best of his ability and glorifying God?"

If your friend answers yes, that an early conversion is a get-out-of-jail-free card for all future transgressions, then you might ask him about 2 Peter 2:20–21 (used above).

If he answers no, then you can say, "I think we agree on this. And in our faith we have more to say about it. Would you like to learn more about our position?"

And if he answers, "I'm not sure," then he has given you the best answer of all because he is acknowledging that there are a hundred ways a person might be truly broken in life, through abuse or cruel experience, that might send him away from the light and that only God can rightly judge what is truly in a man's heart. If this is your friend's answer, then you can again give your agreement and offer to share the additional light the restored gospel brings to this question.

## SCRIPTURE SUPPORT:

| | |
|---|---|
| Matthew 10:22 | He that endureth to the end shall be saved |
| Ephesians 2:8–9 | By grace we are saved, not of works, lest any man should boast |

| | |
|---|---|
| 2 Nephi 25:23 | We know it is by grace we are saved, after all we can do |
| Moroni 10:32 | Deny yourself of all ungodliness and love God . . . then is His grace sufficient for you |

### Question #12: I'm saved too, so why do I need your church?

> **The short answer:** "Because in the Church that Christ has restored to the earth, there is so much more to learn and so many more ways to become closer to Him and to grow and feel more of His love. May I give you an example?"

Most of those who ask you this question will have had at least a little religious training and perhaps a great deal of it. If they respond without enthusiasm to your short answer, it may mean one of the following:

- They sincerely believe that their focus on the saving grace of Jesus Christ is really all that's necessary.
- They view the extras to which you refer as, at best, unnecessary distractions from the purity of Christ's grace, or at worst, evidence of evil and cultish beliefs inspired by man or Satan but not by God.
- They enjoy using their saved condition as a get-out-of-jail-free card that allows them to feel good about the state of their soul while absolving them from the need for any acts of discipleship. To acknowledge there's more would be to recognize the need to *do* more—a step they may not be inclined to take.

By offering to give your friend an example of the added truths found within The Church of Jesus Christ of Latter-day Saints, such as the Book of Mormon or temple ordinances, you may create a level of curiosity that will cause them to consider that there may be something more to their religious experience that would be of benefit to them.

Please consider carefully the importance of the phrase *benefit to them*. It's been my experience that we are sometimes too quick to present the soul-expanding doctrines of the restored gospel as a long list of spiritual gotta-do's, as if the only way to motivate our questioning friends is to appeal to their sense of duty and obligation. As a motivator for personal change, duty pales in comparison to desire. I am much more likely to pursue a new path if I *want* to than if I am being nagged that I *have* to.

Compare the following messages. They teach the same doctrine but approach it from opposite directions:

### THE TEMPLE

The restored gospel allows us to be sealed together as families both on earth and in the eternities. This has brought great peace to my soul, especially when times are hard.

OR

Temple ordinances are required for eternal progression. If you choose not to qualify for these blessings, you are potentially putting your soul in jeopardy.

### THE WORD OF WISDOM

The Lord's law of health helps us live happier, more energetic, and longer lives. It frees us from physical addictions. It is a great blessing.

OR

The Lord's law of health means you must give up your coffee, tea, and cigarettes. You can't be baptized until you do.

### LATTER-DAY PROPHETS

The prophet helps us understand God's plan for our lives. This brings a deep sense of purpose, happiness, and contentment. It helps me feel confident in the presence of God (see Doctrine and Covenants 121:45).

OR

We consider the prophet to be the voice of God to the earth today. He tells us what we need to do, and we do it. It's our duty as disciples. It is one of the ways we honor God.

Meanwhile, in your ward last Sunday, you may have been reminded about your home or visiting teaching. Consider which of the following two approaches would best motivate you to visit your families?

Brethren, when we go home teaching and share His love through something as simple as delivering a message and asking if we can be of help, it's easy to feel the Lord's Spirit and approval. Home teaching has made me a better man. My wife thinks so too.

OR

Brethren, you hold the priesthood, and home teaching is part of that. It is a duty and obligation. If you aren't doing something this basic, can you really say that you're meeting the requirements of a temple recommend?

So if your friend is willing to let you share an example of how the restored gospel has expanded your knowledge of Heavenly Father and Jesus Christ, be careful to show him how he can benefit from all of our extra light. We must do more than simply say, in effect, "Here's what you have to do, and now that you know it, you have to do it."

## SCRIPTURE SUPPORT:

| | |
|---|---|
| 1 Corinthians 2:9 | Eye hath not seen . . . the things which God hath prepared for those who love him |
| Doctrine and Covenants 121:33 | As well might man try to stop the Missouri River as to stop the Almighty from pouring knowledge upon the heads of the Latter-day Saints |
| Doctrine and Covenants 121:46 | The Holy Ghost shall be thy constant companion . . . and without compulsory means it shall flow unto thee forever |

# QUESTIONS ABOUT PRIESTHOOD AUTHORITY

*Question #13: Do you worship Joseph Smith?*

**The short answer:** "No, but we consider him to be a prophet of equal stature to Moses or Isaiah. We hold him in great respect, but we do not worship him."

## SCRIPTURE SUPPORT:

| | |
|---|---|
| 2 Nephi 3:9 | Joseph Smith shall be great like unto Moses (see the entire prophesy in verses 3–22) |
| Doctrine and Covenants 135:3 | Joseph Smith has done more, save Jesus Christ, for the salvation of men in the world than any other man that ever lived in it |

One of my sister missionaries once reported being asked by an investigator if it was true that we believed Joseph Smith to be a literal descendent of Jesus Christ. She assured him that was not the case.

You hear strange things in the mission field. At least this person had the courage to ask the question so he could learn the truth.

## Question #14: Why do you need a prophet?

We need to be careful in answering this question that we do not give offense to our Protestant friends who have a vastly different view of the need for priesthood authority. Their entire branch of Christianity was founded on the idea that no such need exists.

The Protestant movement in the Christian church (known generally as the Reformation) began in the early sixteenth century with Martin Luther, John Calvin, and other reformers. They argued that the Holy See of the Catholic Church had become corrupt. They rejected the authority of the pope and the priesthood in general, believing that a man seeking salvation could confidently approach God directly and that no priestly intermediary was necessary.

Seen in this light, the LDS claim of the value of a prophet and the need for ordinances performed under the authority of the priesthood sounds a great deal like the doctrine Protestants have spent the last five centuries rejecting.

Also, many of our Protestant friends are baffled by our level of organization. Some Protestant religions (for example, the Southern Baptists) have a very loose central structure. Except for a few central core beliefs, each Southern Baptist church is pretty much free to run itself as it sees fit. This lack of structure—which would seem to be a recipe for confusion to a Latter-day Saint—is understood to be a cherished blessing to those who have embraced that religious culture and tradition. Followers are free to move as they see fit from congregation to congregation, and even from sect to sect, in their search for a church that best meets their spiritual needs. Consequently, many Protestants believe that all Protestant churches teaching a belief in Christ and the power of His grace are of equal saving power. This allows the individual to discover Christ on his own terms and follow the Master in his own way. To your Protestant friends, this religious tradition is an honored birthright and the core of his experience with Jesus Christ.

Meanwhile, your Catholic friends may also take offense to your claims that papal authority was lost in the Catholic Church due to the abuse of power and pastoral hypocrisy so severe that Christ utterly withdrew His endorsement and authority from the Catholic Church as an institution.

All of which is simply to say that we need to be careful about how we discuss this subject that will be controversial to nearly everyone with whom we speak.

**The short answer:** "We are a unified, worldwide church. The prophet directs the work of the Church as a whole and encourages us all to be true disciples of Christ."

This is when a short answer serves your purpose well. In a few words, you've laid the groundwork for the follow-up questions that will help you understand the needs and interests of your friend.

## SCRIPTURE SUPPORT:

| | |
|---|---|
| Amos 3:7 | The Lord God will reveal his secrets to his prophets |
| Ephesians 2:20 | The church is built upon the foundation of apostles and prophets |
| Matthew 4:17–22 | Jesus begins to call the disciples who will become His Apostles |
| Matthew 10 | Jesus instructs the Apostles to preach the gospel, minister to the world, and heal the sick |
| Acts 1:21–26 | Matthias is chosen to fill a vacancy in the Quorum of the Twelve Apostles |
| Acts 10:9–16 | As the senior Apostle, Peter receives the revelation to preach the gospel to the Gentiles |

### Question #15: Why do you need a church leader to always tell you what to do?

This gets to the heart of the culturally hard-wired problem many Protestants have with priesthood authority (see Question #14)—that we (Mormons) impose an earthly intermediary between ourselves and God. A misunderstanding of the doctrine of the priesthood makes the Church a nonstarter for many.

And because we don't understand the depth of the concern our Protestant friends have about this question, we often don't answer it in a way that meets their needs. In other words, we fumble it.

> **The short answer:** "We believe that God inspires the prophet and other Church leaders to direct the Church in general. And, just like you, I have access to a local pastor—we call him a bishop—who I can turn to for council and advice. But when I need answers in my own life, I turn directly to God in prayer, and He answers me individually, without anyone in the middle."

This may seem obvious to you, but it is a real concern to many. This answer should help resolve some of your friend's concerns.

If he asks for more clarification, you need to be ready to explain our position of the role of the priesthood in communication from God. It may sound complicated, but it's not. It was explained beautifully and simply by Elder Dallin H. Oaks in his October 2010 general conference address, "Two Lines of Communication."

Elder Oaks explains that there are two lines of communication employed by the Savior as He communicates to man—the personal line and the priesthood line. When Christ wants to communicate to the Church as a whole, He inspires the prophet and the Quorum of the Twelve. In this way, He is using the priesthood line. When Christ wants to communicate directly to me, He sends inspiration directly to me through the Holy Ghost. In this way, He is using the personal line.

These two lines of communication between God and man allow for order to be maintained: the Church as a whole receives direction, and each of us are inspired to know how we can best navigate through life's challenges.

If you will take the time to carefully read through Elder Oaks's talk, you will be able to confidently explain our position in a way that will help resolve your friend's concerns.

## SCRIPTURE SUPPORT:

The "two lines of communication" doctrine is well supported in the Holy Bible.

| | |
|---|---|
| Acts 10:9–16 | As the senior Apostle, Peter receives the revelation to preach the gospel to the Gentiles (the priesthood line) |
| Acts 11:1–18 | Peter declares that the Church will not require circumcision of new converts (the priesthood line) |
| 1 Samuel 1:9–20 | Hannah asks the Lord for a son and is blessed with Samuel (the personal line) |
| Matthew 2:13 | The Lord tells Joseph in a dream to take Mary and the infant Jesus to Egypt (the personal line) |

## Question #16: Why can't women hold the priesthood in your church?

The expansion of life opportunities for women throughout the world has been a blessing for men and women alike. All have benefitted from women of talent and training who have excelled in their chosen fields. Long gone are the days where anyone seriously suggests that women have no place outside a few traditional and narrowly defined paths in life.

There are still battles to be fought. In some corners of the world, progress for women has come slowly and grudgingly. In Western societies we look with dismay at the restrictions in conduct and appearance imposed on women in some other cultures, restrictions that are often justified in the name of religion. But even in First World countries, economic inequalities continue. And within our homes, surveys show the work of homemaking remains unequally shared.[26]

When inequalities are discovered, those making the discoveries rarely remain silent. Instead, their findings fly throughout the world. Women as a whole have been blessed when the darker corners of the world have been illuminated and inequities have been exposed.

In this spirit comes the occasional public debate over the role of women in the Church. To those not of our faith, it looks like a simple argument: The male-dominated Church leadership refuses to relinquish its power, leaving women in a subordinate role in both Mormon leadership and in the homes of Church members. In the process, critics say, centuries-old social stereotypes are forced upon modern women in the name of religion. It is, they argue, fundamentally unfair.

And it is an argument that occasionally even finds a home in the heart of some Church members.

Absent from that argument is an understanding of Church doctrine on the subject and an awareness of the ever-expanding role of women in the councils of the Church in wards, stakes, and general leadership. For those who foster the debate within the Church, doctrines are either misunderstood or considered the perpetuation of uninspired cultural traditions that unfairly restrict the progress of women in this life and the hereafter.

---

26   There is no shortage of studies on this subject, and they all come to the same conclusion. For example, a 2012 study by the British Institute for Public Policy Research found that in 8 out of 10 couples surveyed, women did "substantially" more housework than their partners.

In either case, the ultimate answer to the question of why women do not hold the priesthood—because that's the way God has ordained things—falls on ears that are not well tuned to hear the harmonies of heaven. The critics misunderstand. And, as in so many areas of life, what we do not understand, we criticize.

But if you are asked to explain why women do not hold the priesthood, you can confidently respond with a fuller answer than the "God doesn't want us to" argument. It's ironic, after all, that we may be criticized for not allowing women to hold the priesthood, yet women are administering gospel programs to segments of Church membership in a greater degree than any other church of which I am aware. Outsiders who find fault with us make the incorrect assumption that only those who hold the priesthood run things in the Church. Ask any overworked Relief Society, Primary, or Young Women president at the ward, stake, and general level about their responsibilities—along with their accompanying counselors and board members—and they will share with you the long hours spent pleading with the Lord for inspiration on how to proceed with the leadership burdens placed on their shoulders.

So if you are asked, here is an idea for an answer that might help guide your friend to a better understanding of the powerful role women play in the Church.

**The short answer:** "Well, first of all, you shouldn't think that the Church is only led by the priesthood. Women are represented in decision-making councils throughout the Church, from Salt Lake City down to our local congregation. Women in the Church preach, teach, provide counsel to other members, and hold positions of significant responsibility. Yes, men hold the priesthood because it models the church Christ Himself organized. But in the Church and in our lives, Mormon men and women are absolutely equally engaged. If you are interested, you should come and see for yourself how it all works."

Some, of course, will be unwilling to surrender their beliefs that Mormon women are kept under the thumb of the men, refusing to see any evidence to the contrary. In responding, the seed of your testimony may fall on stony ground. But as you do your best to plant the seed, you must, as always, rely on the Lord for the harvest.

**SCRIPTURE SUPPORT:**

In the church He established, Jesus chose twelve Apostles, all of whom are men. Our church, which mirrors the church He established in both organization and authority, does the same.

| | |
|---|---|
| Matthew 10 | Jesus commissions His Apostles to preach the gospel and heal the sick. None are women. |

Jesus showed great respect and deference towards women. He did not, however, call them to serve in priesthood positions.

| | |
|---|---|
| John 11:5, 17–46 | Jesus loved Mary and Martha. When their brother Lazarus dies, He shows tenderness and compassion for the sisters |
| Luke 10:38–42 | When the Savior is teaching, He makes a special effort to make sure that the women are allowed to listen |
| Matthew 28:1–10 | Following His Resurrection, Jesus appears first to women—Mary Magdalene and Mary the sister of Lazarus |

### Question #17: Do you really believe that you're the only true church in the world?

When our nonmember friends discover that we believe our church is "the only true and living church upon the face of the whole earth" (Doctrine and Covenants 1:30), we cannot be surprised when they respond with, at best, a raised eyebrow or, at worst, anger at our hubris.

The disconnect occurs because of a misunderstanding. The phrase *only true and living church* refers solely to the authority of the Melchizedek Priesthood, which we believe exists only in The Church of Jesus Christ of Latter-day Saints.[27] However, the lack of the true priesthood in other churches does not stop faithfully humble believers from being blessed, often richly, by those gospel truths we all share in common. The so-called Golden Rule, for example, is taught straightforwardly in every one of the world's major religions.[28]

But a detailed explanation of the characteristics of the Melchizedek Priesthood is probably not what your friend wants to hear in response to this question. This short answer may better meet your friend's needs.

**The short answer:** "We believe that all churches contain a great deal of truth. But we believe that when the Savior restored His Church, He restored additional truths that had been lost from the earth for centuries. We invite everyone to bring us the great truths they possess and let us add to them, to everyone's benefit."

### SCRIPTURE SUPPORT:

Ephesians 4:5                    One lord, one faith, one baptism

---

27  For example, consider these remarks concerning the priesthood from "Excerpts from Recent Addresses of President Gordon B. Hinckley," *Ensign*, August 1998: "This [is a] remarkable and wonderful gift of authority in these great latter days. . . . Without it, we have nothing. It is the power of governance in the Church. It is the authority to speak in the name of God."

28  For example, Buddhism: "Hurt not others in ways that you yourself would find hurtful" (Udana-Varga 5,1) or Islam: "No one of you is a believer until he desires for his brother that which he desires for himself" (Sunnah). For a more exhaustive list of the Golden Rule in world religions, see www.teachingvalues. com, "The Universality of the Golden Rule in the World's Religions."

| 1 Corinthians 14:33 | God is not the author of confusion |
| Matthew 18:18 | Whatsoever ye shall bind on earth shall be bound in heaven |

## ADDITIONAL SUPPORT:

"Let me say that we appreciate the truth in all churches and the good which they do. We say to the people, in effect, you bring with you all the good that you have, and then let us see if we can add to it. That is the spirit of this work. That is the essence of our missionary service."[29]

---

29   Quoted in "Excerpts from Recent Addresses of President Gordon B. Hinckley," *Ensign*, August 1998.

# QUESTIONS ABOUT SOCIAL ISSUES

### *Question #18: How many wives do you have?*

> **The short answer:** "One. And in my experience, that's plenty. And just for the record, it's been more than 120 years since the Church allowed polygamy."

Nothing wrong with a little humor when you can get away with it. But it's always a good idea to remind people that for well over a century the Church has been polygamy free. That's a long time. This answer also helps to remind your friend that the polygamy television shows are in no way connected with the lives of Latter-day Saints.

**SCRIPTURE SUPPORT:**
See the scriptures used in the next question.

### Question #19: Why did the Church ever practice polygamy?

Ah, polygamy.

It's our doctrinal claim to fame. People may not know anything about the Latter-day Saints, but they know there was polygamy in our past, and depending on how closely they read the news and watch cable TV, they may suspect that Mormons are actively involved with it today.

Discussing polygamy gets a knowing wink from men and a cold shoulder from women. It's why the immediate response I get when people discover I'm a Mormon is usually Question #18.

Polygamy was a public part of the Church from 1852 to 1890 and was practiced privately by some members (mostly leaders) for ten to fifteen years before that. After the Church announced the discontinuation of polygamy in 1890, it nevertheless continued on a very small scale for another fourteen years until Joseph F. Smith announced that those involved would be excommunicated—which ended the practice once and for all.[30]

All leering about polygamy aside, if the early Mormons were reaching for acceptance in the world, this wasn't the way to go about it. As the Church began the open practice of polygamy after its relocation to the then-distant Utah Territory, it inflamed passions and incurred the indignation of politicians and American society in general. Abraham Lincoln famously campaigned for the presidency in 1860 in full support of the Republican Party platform calling for the end of "the twin relics of barbarism—slavery and polygamy."[31] In 1862 Lincoln signed the Anti-Bigamy Act, which made polygamy a federal crime; although he earned the respect of Latter-day Saints by deliberately choosing not to enforce it.[32]

---

30    The basics of polygamy in the Church are fairly discussed at lds.org—Gospel Topics—Plural Marriage and Families in Early Utah. A more detailed discussion of the practice of polygamy after the 1890 Manifesto of Wilford Woodruff can be found at mormon-polygamy.org/second manifesto. Following the presentation of the Second Manifesto by Joseph F. Smith on April 6, 1904 in general conference, two Apostles, John W. Taylor and Matthias F. Crowley, were ultimately excommunicated due to their disagreement with the official Church position.

31    See "Republican Party Started Out Anti-Mormon," *Salt Lake Tribune*, February 27, 2012.

32    See Edwin Brown, Richard Collin, *Zion in the Courts*, University of Illinois Press, 2001, 139. This citation includes a quote from Abraham Lincoln, comparing the Church to a log he'd encountered that was "too hard to split, too wet to burn, and too heavy to move, so we plow around it. That's what I intend to do with the Mormons. You go back and tell Brigham Young that if he will let me alone, I will let him alone."

At the time, the moral outrage of the nation toward plural marriage struck the Church as hypocritical to the extreme. In the Mormon view, it was the Gentile society that was and always had been morally corrupt. At least, the paraphrased argument went, we're marrying these women, not indulging in tawdry affairs that mock the sacred nature of the marriage covenant.[33]

Polygamy was never practiced by all Mormons in Utah. Overall, only about 20 percent of Mormons were directly involved in polygamous families. Personal worthiness as assessed by Church leaders, along with some measure of economic viability, was required. The permission of the first wife was required before other wives could be added to the family. Plural marriage was never forced on any participants.[34]

For all its controversy, the Lord's reinstatement of the ancient biblical practice of polygamy at a time when the Church was small in numbers but large in vision was in some ways a blessing to the Saints. It made marriage available to virtually all who desired it, and (not surprisingly) it produced many more Mormons. It's worth remembering that as the Saints began to settle the Salt Lake Valley, they faced difficult odds. The valley was no "land of milk and honey." It was the ultimate fixer-upper. The population growth in the valley due to polygamous unions, along with the arrival of new converts, provided the labor needed to gradually bring the desert to heel.[35]

Still, legal battles between the Church and the United States over the practice of polygamy caused great hardships to members. Wilford Woodruff's Manifesto—now known as Official Declaration 1 in the Doctrine and Covenants—ended the US legal opposition to the Church.

---

33   Consider this fragment from a sermon by President John Taylor, given in the Assembly Hall on Temple Square, February 10, 1884. Speaking of the Gentiles in the Eastern United States with mocking sarcasm, he said, "Their pure souls are very much agonized about . . . impurities which exist among the Mormons. They cannot see or say anything about the licentiousness, the corruption, the foeticide (abortion), the infanticide, the rottenness, hypocrisy, lying, fraud and deception that exits among themselves; but they think we are a very bad people, and in order to purge the nation of so foul a blot, they must all unite to put us down."

34   All statements made in this paragraph originate from James B. Allen and Glen M. Leonard, *The Story of the Latter-day Saints*, 2nd edition, Deseret Book Company, 1992, 287.

35   See lds.org—Gospel Topics—Plural Marriage and Families in Early Utah for a discussion, with lengthy footnotes, of the practical and sociological effects of the polygamy as practiced during the 1850–1890 period.

At the time some felt the Manifesto was politically motivated, but for the rest of his life, Woodruff never wavered from teaching that the Manifesto was divinely inspired.[36]

> **The short answer:** "Well, you probably know that there were times in the Old Testament when the Lord temporarily allowed polygamy. For a period of about fifty years, the Lord officially instituted polygamy among the early Latter-day Saints. A relatively small portion of Church members took part in it. It's a fascinating part of US history, but the Lord rescinded polygamy for the Church in 1890."

## SCRIPTURE SUPPORT:

| | |
|---|---|
| Genesis 16:3 | Sarai gives her servant Hagar to Abraham to be his second wife |
| Genesis 25:1 | Abraham takes another wife, Keturah |
| Genesis 29:21–30 | Laban gives both Rachel and Leah to Jacob to be his wives |
| 2 Samuel 12:7–9 | The prophet Nathan chastises David for having received many wives from the Lord but still turning to Bathsheba |
| Jacob 2:27, 30 | Jacob teaches that monogamy is to be practiced by the Church except for when God temporarily decrees otherwise (for example, to "raise up seed") |

---

36  President Woodruff later said of the divine origin of the Manifesto, "I should have let all the temples go out of our hands; I should have gone to prison myself, and let every other man go there, had not the God of heaven commanded me to do what I did do; and when the hour came that I was commanded to do that, it was all clear to me." See "Excerpts from three addresses by President Wilford Woodruff regarding the Manifesto," immediately following Official Declaration 1.

| Doctrine and Covenants 132:34–36 | The Lord justifies Abraham in veering from monogamy when specifically ordered by the Lord |
| Official Declaration 1 | The Church will no longer endorse or condone plural marriage |

### Question #20: Didn't you once discriminate against black people in your church?

Enough years have passed that an entire generation has grown up without a direct memory of the time when The Church of Jesus Christ of Latter-day Saints prohibited black males from holding the priesthood, and black men and women from entering the temple. The practice was ended in 1978—an event recorded in the Doctrine and Covenants: Official Declaration 2.

During the turbulent civil rights era from the late '50s and '60s, the Church's ban on blacks holding the priesthood led many people of goodwill to denounce the Church as a blatantly racist organization. BYU sports teams were often picketed in protest when visiting other cities.[37]

Speaking personally, I was baptized in 1975. During the time when the missionaries taught me, I prayed to know if the Church was true. I received an answer to my prayers and agreed to baptism. I felt that the Church's ban on blacks receiving the priesthood was a trial that I had to accept on faith. I was uncomfortable with it, but I could not deny the truth of the gospel. Like many millions in the Church, I was prepared to patiently wait for the Lord to change the doctrine as Brigham Young had prophesied would one day come to pass.[38]

Such was the drama of it that I can remember where I was and what I was doing when I heard a 1978 radio news report that began, "The Mormon Church announces a revelation from God!" It explained that the Church had ended the prohibition against blacks receiving the priesthood and temple ordinances.

The news flashed across the world. The Church rejoiced.

During the years leading up to the announcement, from Brigham Young to Spencer W. Kimball, Church leaders and writers occasionally attempted to explain the doctrine without much success. No Church

---

37  See, for example, Jay Drew, "BYU Football: Remembering the Black 14 Protest," *Salt Lake Tribune*, November 6, 2009. The article describes the event and aftermath of the BYU-Wyoming football game of October 18, 1969, when fourteen black Wyoming players were dismissed from the team the day before the game because they insisted on wearing black armbands during the game to protest the Church's ban on blacks holding the priesthood.

38  In 1852, Brigham Young said, the "time will come when they will have the privilege of all we have the privilege of and more" (Brigham Young Papers, Church Archives, February 5, 1852).

President ever offered an explanation of the doctrine that went beyond theories and conjecture. Ultimately, we don't know why the ban was put in place. From the founding of the Church in 1830, black men *were* entitled to receive the priesthood. Then, in 1852, Brigham Young discontinued the practice. President Young's policy remained fixed until 1978.

Since then, the change in the Church has been remarkable. The announcement of Official Declaration 2 in 1978—known unofficially as the Revelation on the Priesthood—has ushered in a new era of Church growth. Throughout the world, black men and women now hold positions of authority in wards, stakes, and temples. As a Church, we believe the Revelation on the Priesthood to be evidence that the Lord continues to reveal "many great and important things pertaining to the Kingdom of God" (Articles of Faith 1:9). At the time of the announcement, most Church members accepted the Lord's will gladly and moved forward. A generation later we continue to move forward at a steadily quickening pace. We do not hide our past, but we invite people to see and judge the Church as it is today, recognizing that the judgments others may apply to the Church in the past are relevant only to the Church in the past. They are not relevant to the actions and deeds of the Church today.[39]

> **The short answer:** "Early in Church history, black men were ordained to the priesthood, but at some point that practice was stopped. The early Church records aren't clear about why. The ban unfortunately continued until 1978, when the Church prophet at the time received a revelation ending it. Today all

---

39    For example, consider this statement from Bruce R. McConkie, from his talk "All Are Alike unto God," given at a CES Religious Educators Symposium, August 18, 1978, "We get our truth and our light line upon line and precept upon precept. We have now had added a new flood of intelligence and light on this particular subject, and it erases all the darkness and all the views and all the thoughts of the past. They don't matter anymore. It doesn't make a particle of difference what anybody ever said about the Negro matter before the first day of June of this year, 1978. It is a new day and a new arrangement, and the Lord has now given the revelation that sheds light out into the world on this subject. As to any slivers of light or any particles of darkness of the past, we forget about them. We now do what meridian Israel did when the Lord said the gospel should go to the Gentiles. We forget all the statements that limited the gospel to the house of Israel, and we start going to the Gentiles."

worthy male members can be ordained to the priesthood, and people of every race may enter the temple. In fact, much of the explosive growth in the Church today is in Africa."

## SCRIPTURE SUPPORT:

The history of the priesthood, as an office that may be held by many, shows a gradual expansion over time. In the Old Testament, the Aaronic, or Levitical, Priesthood was only held by members of the tribe of Levi, one of the twelve tribes of Israel (see 1 Kings 8:4 and Ezra 2:70). This pattern continued at the time of Jesus (see John 1:19).

However, during His ministry, Jesus ordained twelve Apostles, bestowing on them the spiritual power and authority of the Melchizedek Priesthood. The Apostles were all Jews, but they belonged to various tribes of the house of Israel (see Matthew 10).

Following the death and Resurrection of Christ, Peter, the senior Apostle, assumed leadership of the Church, and he received the revelation to take the gospel and the priesthood to the Gentiles (see Acts 10:9–48).

Seen in this light, access to the priesthood is one of gradual unfolding and expansion, now at last made complete in this final dispensation of the gospel (see Official Declaration 2).

### Question #21: Are you against abortion?

Part of the beauty of the gospel as taught in The Church of Jesus Christ of Latter-day Saints is its simplicity. For centuries man has wrestled with the great questions of life: Where did I come from? Why am I here? Where am I going? But ask a Primary child those questions, and you'll hear answers that confound the wise:

"I am a child of God."

"I lived with Heavenly Father as a spirit before I was born."

"I came to earth to learn how to obey God's commandments."

"One day I will return to Heavenly Father and live with Him forever."

In the Church we understand that our life on earth is an essential part of the spiritual progression for which we fought in the premortal realm. The denial of life to God's spirits frustrates His plans for His children and impedes an individual's power to progress.

As Mormons, we are therefore unapologetically opposed to abortion, and we work with kindness to help those with unwanted pregnancies to find loving alternatives to that dark and grim procedure.

> **The short answer:** "The Church believes in the sanctity of human life, and I agree with that. We believe that abortion for personal or social convenience is a sin. In the Church, members who are a party to an abortion under those conditions can lose their membership."

If your friend asks something along the line of, "But what about the plight of a poor or desperate mother?" you can respond by explaining LDS Family Services and how unwed mothers are able to give birth and have their children adopted by families who are able to provide the infant with a loving and nurturing home. You should also be ready to explain that a nonmember involved in an abortion may still join the Church but will require additional counseling before doing so.

### SCRIPTURE SUPPORT:

| | |
|---|---|
| Jeremiah 1:5 | Before I formed thee in the belly I knew thee (reality of the premortal world) |

Doctrine and Covenants 59:6    Thou shalt not kill, nor do anything like unto it

See also *The Family: A Proclamation to the World.* Paragraph three discusses the premortal life and the plan of salvation. Paragraph five states, "We affirm the sanctity of life and its importance in God's eternal plan."

See also the article on abortion at lds.org—Gospel Topics—Abortion.

### *Question #22: Why do Mormons have so many children?*

This is a tender topic for many Church members, touching as it does on some of our deepest feelings about happiness and our closeness to God.

To my knowledge, only Mormons share the understanding of parenthood as a partnership with God by bringing His spirit sons and daughters into the world so they can be taught correct principles along their unique path of eternal progression.

Social research validates the basic premise of this question at least in the United States. Church members *do* have more children than society at large. According to a study conducted in 2010, the birth rate among LDS women exceeded the national birthrate by about a third—around 80 births per 1,000 Mormon women per year, compared to around 60 births per 1,000 women per year in the United States as a whole.[40]

But it's also worth noting that that the higher birthrate among LDS women does not apply to those who are not married. A 2014 study showed that in the United States about 35 percent of babies are born to unwed mothers. In Utah, with its dominant Mormon culture, only about 15 percent of babies are born to unwed mothers.[41]

In an age when the cultural goals of advanced societies seems to be centered around moving through life with as few encumbrances as possible, the LDS focus on the simple joys of home and family life may seem out of date, anachronistic, quaint, or simply strange. Nevertheless, a wide variety of social indicators point to the validity of the Mormon way of life—that despite challenges, traditional values of clean living, hard work, and a family-centered focus produce happier and healthier children and adults.[42]

**The short answer**: "Well, you're right—the birthrate among Church members does run higher than society at large. It

---

40   See "US Fertility Rates Tops the US Charts," *Deseret News*, November 7, 2010.

41   See "Utah has nation's lowest rate of births to unwed moms," *Salt Lake Tribune*, August 9, 2014.

42   See, for example, "Mormons among Nation's Healthiest, Researchers Say," *Los Angeles Times*, April 26, 1997, and the *Encyclopedia of Mormonism* at http://eom.byu.edu/index.php/Social_Characteristics for an exhaustive list of social research findings demonstrating Mormons as a whole to exceed national averages in physical health, happiness, and mental health.

might be because we believe bringing children into a loving home is one of life's greatest blessings. Some husbands and wives choose to have larger families. It can be challenging, but it can also be very rewarding."

## SCRIPTURE SUPPORT:

| | |
|---|---|
| Psalm 127:3–5 | Children are an heritage of the Lord |
| Proverbs 17:6 | Grandchildren are the glory of old men |

## ADDITIONAL SUPPORT:

From *The Family: A Proclamation to the World*

Paragraph 4: "We declare that God's commandment for His children to multiply and replenish the earth remains in force"

Paragraph 7: "Happiness in family life is most likely to be achieved when founded upon the teachings of the Lord Jesus Christ"

## Question #23: Are you against birth control?

Given the fact that Church members tend to have larger families (see Question #22), some might assume that the Church opposes the use of birth control. Actually, the Church neither supports nor opposes birth control, believing that decisions involving family planning are between the husband, wife, and the Lord.

If LDS families tend to be larger than average (and they do), it is because those families have chosen to have more children, not because they have been forbidden the tools that allow the choice. In making decisions about family size, the Church recognizes that many factors must be carefully and sensitively considered, including the health of the mother and the family's ability to provide a stable and nurturing environment for children. As a result, some LDS families are larger; some are not.

Regardless of family size, the husbands and wives in LDS families I have known tend to have deep faith and a sense of partnership with the Lord in providing loving and welcoming homes for His spirit children who have waited so long to come to earth.

> **The short answer**: "The Church recognizes that the decisions involved in planning a family are private matters between a husband and wife. In general, we believe bringing children into the world is one of life's greatest blessings, but the details of how that is accomplished are not the concern of the Church."

## SCRIPTURE SUPPORT:

Psalm 127:3–5
Children are a gift of the Lord. They are likened to arrows, and "happy is the man who has a quiver full of them."

### Question #24: Are you against premarital sex? Isn't that unrealistic?

I know of no aspect of human existence in which the world has swung further away from the Church than its expression of sexuality. To seriously suggest that men and women can (and should) refrain from sexual activity until marriage and then remain faithful to their spouse for the remainder of their lives is widely considered abnormal, ludicrous, and the stuff of late-night comedy. This may not be surprising, considering that in the United States three-quarters of both men and women have experienced sexual intercourse by their eighteenth birthday.[43]

Popular entertainment portrays sex outside of marriage as an utterly natural part of life. It is difficult to find a romantic-comedy movie in which the couple does not engage in explicit or implied sexual behavior before marriage that would guarantee the need for an extended visit with the bishop in real life.

Meanwhile, the smothering, ubiquitous effects of pornography and what has become its passive acceptance by society at large, adds vast amounts of fuel to the fire. Those who oppose pornography's availability have been rendered powerless to stop it. It's one thing to picket the XXX bookstore on the edge of town, but today's Internet-delivered pornography absolves the user from exposure—until it is discovered by those within the family, often when the consequences from repeated exposure begin to spill into the user's day-to-day relationships.

Make no mistake—the Church's position on sexual expression is so far from the general view of nonmembers as to be not just bad or wrong but utterly irrelevant. Hence this question—which I have been asked more than once: Isn't the Church's position on premarital sexual abstinence simply unrealistic?

There have, of course, always been those who have sought riotous living.[44] Today it has become a lifestyle that is much easier to pursue. For those who profit from marketing "extreme" excitement in all its forms, this must be a golden age. The multiple platforms on which they can peddle their goods are unmatched in human history.

---

43   See www.kinseyinstitute.org/resources/FAQ for statistical research on a variety of sexual topics, including age of first intercourse.

44   See Luke 15:11–32 for the Savior's tale of the prodigal son, who took his inheritance and wasted it all on riotous living.

Meanwhile, we can pull out scripture after scripture decrying society's moral decay,[45] but we must realize that at this particular time in history our efforts will cause many people, perhaps most of them, to see us only as the crazy guy shouting on the street corner or as modern versions of Samuel the Lamanite, calling down from the wall of the city and receiving nothing but abuse in return.[46]

And yet, in the midst of all this cultural scorn for the commandments of God, there are those outside our faith who listen, who consider, and who respond. I have met many of them as they have joined the Church—men and women who have felt the need to keep their inner understanding of right and wrong to themselves because they didn't know where to find others who believe as they do. I have been struck many times by the sense of *relief* many converts feel as they join with us and experience an affirmation that there are others who feel the way they have felt and seek the things they have sought. In joining the Church, they have found—at last—the end of the beginning of their search.

We will, I'm afraid, always be a minority, but that has been understood from the beginning.[47] Nevertheless, the truth of God is not noise in the wind—it is gravity. Those closest to its center feel its pull most strongly. Those farther away, less so. Yet gravity holds the planets in place and the stars in alignment to the blessing of us all, whether we notice it or not.

The good news is that however small we are in comparison to the wider world, there are others outside our Church who join with us in making the apparently audacious claim that sexual abstinence before

---

45  All of 2 Nephi 28 comes to mind, as Nephi thunders against those who call evil good, and good evil, and are lulled by Satan into a state of carnal security, and believe that there is no devil, until he leads them "carefully down to hell." However, a quick check of the topic "Chastity" in the Topical Guide will give you twenty-seven immediate references, along with suggesting ten similar topics which will lead you to dozens more.

46  See the story of Samuel the Lamanite in Helaman 13–15.

47  See, for example, Steven Snow, "Balancing Church History," *New Era*, June 2013. "The true church has always been a minority, and it seems like we've always had a target on our backs. We'll always face adversity, and we might as well get used to that."

marriage is not only possible but practical. We may be in the minority, but we are far from alone.[48]

In the end, there will be many, and they will likely be a majority, who will view our allegiance to the Lord's law of chastity as little more than a quaint curiosity to be observed with a bemused smile through the cultural microscope of the current age. To them we can only state what we believe and hope that the Spirit is able to find a place in their heart to kindle a spark.

> **The short answer:** "We believe that God's commandments don't change even though the attitudes of society do. We believe that sexual relations are to be shared only between a husband and wife who are legally married. Is it unrealistic? Well, even if most people think it's impractical, there are still millions who are living the Lord's standard. It is far from impossible."

## SCRIPTURE SUPPORT:

There are dozens that will serve equally well. The Lord has not been silent on this subject. Here are a few:

| | |
|---|---|
| Alma 41:10 | Wickedness never was happiness |
| 2 Nephi 28:20 | Satan will rage in the hearts of men and stir them up against good |
| Genesis 2:24 | A man shall cleave unto his wife and none else |
| Genesis 39:7–12 | Joseph flees from the sexual advances of Potiphar's wife |
| Titus 2:5 | Be discreet, chaste |
| James 1:27 | Keep yourself unspotted from the world |

---

48  A quick Google search for abstinence-based websites will point you to dozens of sites dedicated to helping youth (and adults) deal with the social tornado of extramarital sex. Waitingtillmarriage.org has a compiled a list of forty-five abstinence-based sites. You can find the list at projects.waitingtillmarriage.org/abstinence-websites. Many are church-based (lower case "c"—not affiliated with the LDS Church), but many are nonreligious. All, though, make the case that sexual abstinence outside of marriage is a possible and practical way to live.

### Question #25: Why don't you accept gay people into your church?

In recent years the Church's oft-misunderstood position toward those with same-gender attraction has become an occasional lightning rod of controversy. The reason for the confusion is that many find our position confusing. Or they simply believe the Church is anti-gay and engages in discriminatory acts toward homosexuals.

In November 2015, the Church found itself on the front pages of the nation's newspapers with a new policy denying infant name blessings and childhood baptisms to children living in homes with same-sex parents or guardians. The new policy also declared that a same-sex relationship between adult Church members is now an automatic trigger for a Church court.

It is an emotional topic, and in the heat of debate, nuances can be lost. In a 144-character Twitter world, there is relentless pressure to simplify, to dumb down, and to reduce every issue to a single, simple-to-follow but often woefully incomplete sentence that may sound good to the ear but does not satisfy the need for understanding. It is the philosophical equivalent of a diet of Twinkies. These tit-for-tat, gotcha-phrase debates produce vastly more heat than light and create more anger than understanding.

This approach to public debate—widely practiced in the world and even sometimes in the general society of the Church—is condemned by the Savior. He straightforwardly taught the Nephites, "Behold, this is not my doctrine, to stir up the hearts of men with anger, one against another; but this is my doctrine, that such things should be done away" (3 Nephi 11:30).

Book of Mormon prophets understood the role of anger in helping unrighteous leaders create a people ready to engage in war.[49] It is not difficult to see those same tactics used today by all sides of the public arena. In the political and cultural battles that make up today's wars,

---

49   Anger has frequently played a key role in creating a public appetite for war. The Book of Mormon gives several examples of this in the lives of Amalekiah (Alma 48:3), Zarahemnah (43:8), and both Coriantumr and Shiz (Ether 15:6). All these were leaders who stirred up their followers to anger against their enemies to justify warfare. If this is a topic that interests you, do a scripture search for "stir up anger," and see how many times it appears.

fighting without full understanding of others' points of view is not seen as a moral weakness. Catchy negative slogans seem to be all we need to pass judgment on those with whom we appear to disagree. We fight to win rather than listen to understand. Reaching out in love to truly understand a different heart may be noble in theory, but come on, who really has the time for that kind of thing?

In this climate, the so-called debate over the attitude of the Church toward those with same-sex attraction fits perfectly into the War of the Ten-Second Sound Bites:

"The Church discriminates against gays."

"Read the Bible. Homosexuality is a sin."

"People should be able to love whoever they want to love."

"It's Adam and Eve, not Adam and Steve."

"Mormons are stuck in the past."

"Gay rights are part of the liberal agenda to destroy America."

And on and on.

In late 2012 Church leaders launched a website, mormonsandgays. org, to try and cut through the shouting with a voice of calm and reason. With love and compassion it points out that

- Christ loves His children equally, regardless of their sexual orientation.
- Men and women do not choose to be homosexuals.
- Same-gender attraction is NOT a sin (acting on it is).
- Homosexuals who abide by the same rules of moral conduct as the rest of the Church may be baptized, hold Church callings, and receive temple ordinances.
- Church members are obligated to demonstrate love, compassion, and service to all people, including those with same-gender attraction.
- While the Church does not endorse gay marriage, it supports nondiscrimination laws in other areas of public policy involving gays, such as hiring and housing.[50]

As for the policies denying baptism to children in same-gender parent homes, the Church believes that young children should not have to choose between their parents and the Church, which their baptismal covenant would require them to do. (This is the same policy, by the way, that the Church has applied to children growing up in polygamous homes for generations.) As for a child-naming blessing, the same logic applies:

---

50 See mormonnewsroom.org, "Church Supports Nondiscrimination Ordinances," November 10, 2009.

the blessing triggers a membership record, assigning home teachers, and an expectation of a life in the Church—all very difficult in a home so significantly at odds with Church doctrine.[51]

On the site mormonsandgays.org, the Church acknowledges there's still much work to be done—not only in educating the world about the Church's position but in educating members of the Church to respond in a more Christlike way. On the front page of the website we read,

> There is no change in the Church's position of what is morally right. But what is changing—and what needs to change—is to help Church members respond sensitively and thoughtfully when they encounter same-sex attraction in their own families, among other Church members, or elsewhere.[52]

The Church's position on the physical expression of same-gender attraction is fully contained in the Lord's law of chastity, which is that sexual relations are to be expressed only between a man and woman who are legally married. Men and women who together engage in adultery or fornication are breaking the *same commandment* as homosexual men and women who engage in sexual acts with members of their own gender.

Keeping the law of chastity for those without a spouse is certainly challenging for homosexuals and heterosexuals alike, but it is possible, as faithful, single adult members of the Church demonstrate daily as they move forward in their lives with faith, strength, and courage.

**The short answer:** "Actually, we do accept gay people into the Church, and they live God's commandments just as we all do. One of those commandments is what we call the law of chastity, which is that sexual relations are to be shared only between a husband and wife who are legally married. Gay men and women in the Church live by the same moral code as the rest of us. Same-gender sexual relations break the *same commandment* as premarital or extramarital sexual relationships between men and women."

---

51   To see a detailed explanation of this policy, see Elder D. Todd Christofferson's interview on mormonnewsroom.org, "Church Provides Context on Handbook Changes Affecting Same-Sex Marriages," November 6, 2015.

52   See the front page of mormonsandgays.org. The quote is part of the text but is not attributed to a specific writer.

## SCRIPTURE SUPPORT:

Sexual relations between those of the same gender is a sin.

| | |
|---|---|
| Leviticus 18:22 | Same-gender sexual acts condemned |
| Romans 1:24–27 | Same-gender sexual acts described as an act of dishonor to the individual's own body |
| 1 Corinthians 6:9–11 | Same-gender sex acts condemned on equal terms with adultery and fornication between men and women, but repentance is possible |

The gospel imperative to love all mankind

| | |
|---|---|
| Matthew 22:37–39 | Love the Lord with your heart, soul, and mind, and love your neighbor as yourself |
| John 13:34 | A commandment to love one another as He loves us |
| 1 Nephi 11:17 | Even though he doesn't know the meaning of all things, Nephi knows that God loves His children |

## ADDITIONAL SUPPORT:

"With love and understanding the Church reaches out to all God's children, including our gay and lesbian brothers and sisters."[53]

"God's universal fatherhood and love charges each of us with an innate and reverent acknowledgment of our shared human dignity. We are to love one another. We are to treat each other with respect as brothers and sisters and fellow children of God, no matter how much we may differ from one another."[54]

---

53  From the box insert "Where the Church Stands" on mormonsandgays.org.

54  Taken from a statement from Church leadership, October 12, 2010, explaining the Church's position on same-sex attraction. The entire statement can be found at http://www.mormonnewsroom.org/article/church-mormon-responds-to-human-rights-campaign-petition-same-sex-attraction.

### Question #26: *Why don't you wear popular clothes?*

As every parent of a daughter looking for a prom dress knows, it can be difficult to find clothes in today's world that meet the standards of modesty of The Church of Jesus Christ of Latter-day Saints. Our standards are simple to state but hard to execute on the dress racks of most stores. We seek to avoid immodest clothing, defined as follows: "Immodest clothing is any clothing that is tight, sheer, or revealing in any other manner."[55]

Our standards are the same for both young and adult women and for both young and adult men. In general this includes covered shoulders and no shorts above the knee. Men and women who wear the temple garment should wear clothes that cover the garment without adjustment.

On the ever-swinging pendulum of fashion, this puts us squarely between the bikini beaches of Southern California and the hijabs of Muslims. For us, it is a comfortable place to be. It allows for wide latitude in expression without the pressure to display our bodies as if we were decorating our temples with carnival rides and midway games. It also keeps us from falling into the traps of come-and-go fads that drain the wallets and patience of parents and teenagers alike.

When these standards need enforcement—whether at the sacrament table or a stake dance—loving leaders gently provide guidance as necessary. But it isn't (or shouldn't be) necessary for Church fashion police to dictate our wardrobes. We follow the Lord's standard of modesty because we know it comes from His love for us, and we seek to return that love to Him. It should never appear that we are dressing to earn the attention and approval of others by displaying our body. No attention or approval gained from that approach is of any true value. The Lord knows that, but it has never been an easy lesson for His children to learn. So the Lord's standards for modesty allow us to properly express our individuality while allowing us to focus less on each others' bodies and more on our minds, spirits, and hearts—the only true measures of any man's or woman's worth.

**The short answer:** "We believe that basic modesty is an underappreciated virtue in today's world for both men and women. We think it would be a good thing for society if we

---

55   From *For the Strength of Youth*, "Dress and Appearance," italics added.

were all a little less obsessed with our bodies. We hope to be recognized for what we are inside and not just judged for what we could put on public display."

## SCRIPTURE SUPPORT:

| | |
|---|---|
| Genesis 3:21 | God makes coats of skins for Adam and Eve to cover their nakedness |
| 1 Corinthians 6:19 | Your body is the temple of God; it belongs to God |
| 1 Timothy 2:9 | Dress modestly and avoid costly clothing |

### Question #27: Why don't you have any tattoos/body piercings/cool hair coloring?

When we talk about tattoos, piercings, and hair colors that defy nature, we are ultimately talking about fads. Fads come in all types of colors, traits, and trends. They show up in clothes, hairstyles, and unusual behavior—everything from Depression-era dance marathons to the phone-booth stuffing of the fifties. Through the years we've moved from flower children to valley girls, from saggy pants to Tickle Me Elmo, and from flash mobs to the Harlem Shake.

In the end, fads are usually mindless and, if we're being honest, more than a little dumb, but at the time they seem important and relevant. The best thing to be said about fads is that they are temporary. They flare up, burn brightly in the social order for a time, then disappear until they resurface as an object of mockery by the children of those who remember it all with head-shaking fondness. We see the pictures of the seventies' fashions and mutton-chop sideburns, and wonder, "What were they thinking?" Those who lived during those times may look at their own pictures and wonder the same thing.

But fads have always been something from which we can easily recover—just another brief run of social foolishness, inevitably cured by changing your hairstyle or sending a box of your what-was-I-thinking wardrobe off to Deseret Industries or the Salvation Army. But then came the fad of tattoos.

The popularity of tattoos has exploded over the last generation—creating a $1.6 billion yearly industry. The numbers are convincing: As of 2013, only 14 percent of Americans have a tattoo, but for those between eighteen and forty the number hovers just below 40 percent for both men and women.[56] And unlike other fads involving personal appearance, once inked into human skin, tattoos aren't going anywhere. At least not without a fight. Tattoo removal typically requires 6–8 sessions scheduled about 7 weeks apart, at a cost of $100–250 per session.[57]

---

56   From the Pew Research Center, 2013. Cited on statisticbrain.com/tattoo-statistics. Interestingly 35 percent of those with tattoos said their tattoo makes them feel sexier. Only 5 percent said it made them feel more intelligent.

57   There are multiple websites that quote prices for tattoo removal, number of sessions needed, etc. These numbers are a general average the author found in mid-2014.

Recognizing the faddish nature of tattoos, body piercings, and other forms of extreme appearance,[58] Church leaders have long counseled against such practices and against tattoos in particular.[59]

But what of those who received tattoos before making the decision to be baptized? For decades, Church members have been conditioned to see tattoos as a social and spiritual negative—something to be avoided—and sometimes we have extended that avoidance not just to tattoos but to the people who wear them. And now many in the Church must wrestle with an uncomfortable truth: because so many people in the world today have tattoos, many of those joining the Church have them too.

There is no gracious way to say this. I have seen instance after instance of Church members refusing to fully accept tattooed new members. Not that their refusal is outright, but I have seen judgmental members dish out a frosty warmth and pained handshake to those who are "tatted up." And after our converts receive this unaccepting acceptance for a few weeks or months, they tend to drift away. Like anyone, they aren't likely to stay long where they're not wanted. Then the members offer a few tsk-tsks, say, "Well, he obviously didn't have a testimony anyway," and return to their supremely comfortable all-is-well vision of Zion (see 2 Nephi 28:21).

Such behavior is obviously hypocritical. If the new member cleans up well, we extend our welcome regardless of the unseen emotional and spiritual scars he brings from his time in the world. But let him show a visible "scar," and we are presented with something to judge. And humans, even Mormons, tend to have an appallingly poor record of judging righteous judgment.

As the distance between the Church and the world widens and continues to widen, our investigators must cross a wider gulf to come

---

58    In the Church's pamphlet *For the Strength of Youth*, young people are counseled to "avoid being extreme or inappropriately casual in clothing, hairstyle, and behavior."

59    See for example this statement from Gordon B. Hinckley, "Great Shall Be the Peace of Thy Children," general conference, October 2000: "I cannot understand why any young man—or young woman for that matter—would wish to undergo the painful process of disfiguring the skin with various multicolored representations of people, animals, and various symbols. . . . Fathers, caution your sons against having their bodies tattooed. They may resist your talk now, but the time will come when they will thank you. A tattoo is graffiti on the temple of the body."

to us than ever before in the history. To do so they must demonstrate a spiritual courage, strength, and heroism that would put many of us to shame. A common theme I hear as I talk with those joining the Church is that they come to us to be *healed*. They sense the power of Christ's atoning sacrifice and its potential to make them feel whole and to feel true worth—perhaps for the first time in their lives. And so they come to us, carrying with them the scars they have received in the world. Many of those scars are unseen, but some are very visible. The tattoos we see on our new members are merely the physical scars that must unavoidably tag along with their searching spirits as they seek healing from the Master's hand.

What will we do with such members as they join with us in increasing numbers? We will hug them and hold them close to our hearts. We will support them as they receive their first callings and sustain them when they are called to be elders quorum and Relief Society presidents. We will accompany them to the temple. We will work shoulder to shoulder with them as we all push forward the great cause of Zion. And when they are called as bishops and stake presidents, it will be our pleasure to receive their counsel and direction, made all the wiser for their depth of knowledge of the human experience.

I realize that this long—let's be honest—rant does not directly answer the question of why Church members aren't lining up for tattoos and body piercings, but when we're asked this question, we must be careful not to imply that those who already have such markings are not welcome in the Church—something that could easily be inferred if our tone becomes condescending or judgmental as we talk of the need to keep our physical temples pure and clean. The message to your friend, especially if he already has a tattoo or two under his shirt, will come through loud and clear. *Oh, then that makes me already unclean. I'm already disqualified from ever being a member of your Church.*

It is true that we unapologetically and strongly counsel against receiving tattoos, body piercings, and displaying extremes in personal appearance. As with immodest clothing (see Question #26), these extremes draw attention to our bodies instead of our spiritual selves and tend to, in varying degrees, desecrate the radiant and beautiful physical temples of our spirits given to us by a loving Heavenly Father. But those who have gone through life without the knowledge of these sacred principles can hardly be condemned for failing to obey a commandment they never received. This is why missionaries teach the gospel—to teach commandments so that mankind can be blessed by God as they receive and live the new knowledge. In the process of their progress, it is our privilege to reflect the pure love of Jesus Christ to all He has called out of the world, whatever their situation, and to welcome them in full and unreserved fellowship into God's happy family.

> **The short answer:** "Like Paul in the Holy Bible, we believe that our bodies are temples of God for our spirits. We think the way God made us is just fine. People who have tattoos can join the Church, of course, but as Church members we just don't get involved with these kinds of fads."

## SCRIPTURE SUPPORT:

| | |
|---|---|
| Leviticus 19:28 | Ye shall not make any cuttings in your flesh, neither print any marks upon you |
| 1 Corinthians 3:16–17 | Know ye not that ye are a temple of God? |

**Question #28: Why do you have a problem with watching movies, TV shows, and videos or listening to music that everyone else likes just because they have some sex or violence or bad language in them?**

What is the purpose of artistic expression? To see beyond the surface and get at the deeper meanings of life? To lift and ennoble? To entertain? To provide an alternative to the drudgery of life? To create something that is memorable, thought provoking, and beautiful? To make money?

Yes.

It is all those things and more. Shakespeare explored universal themes of love, happiness, vanity, the corruption of power, redemption, and the pursuit of life's deeper meanings in ways that still inspire us. But for Shakespeare, writing plays was about more than creating art—it was about creating an income. Shakespeare sought to touch the soul, but he also had to sell tickets. So the same writer who gave us King Lear also gave us the leering Falstaff, the bawdy and debauched companion of both kings and women of questionable repute.[60]

Those whose inner spark drives them to the creative arts for their life's work must all face this eternal tug-of-war: I want to create work that has true merit, but I also have to pay the bills. So I must balance my own artistic vision with what the public will accept, enjoy, and ultimately spend money to consume.

---

60  For example, from *Henry IV*, part 1, scene 2: "And now am I, if a man should speak truly, little better than one of the wicked," and (speaking of drinking), "'Tis my vocation; 'tis no sin for a man to labor in his vocation." In act 2, scene 2, his friend, Prince Henry, describes him as so fat that "Falstaff sweats to death, and lards the earth as he walks along."

In observing the astounding levels of sexual and violent content in movies, broadcast and cable television shows, books, radio, magazines, music, and the Internet, modern Church leaders have seen evidence of a Satan-inspired effort to corrupt the hearts and souls of the audiences.[61]

Those in the entertainment industry see it differently. In a free-enterprise system, their goal is simple—to turn a profit and maximize value to stockholders. And like hucksters who peddle to the lowest common denominator of every age, they're not particular about how they do it. If, in the process of generating profits, programming and music producers serve Satan's ambitions, they are simply doing what has always been done. Satan's purposes and the quest for profits have always been able to find a happy companionship throughout history.[62] The only difference today is that the means of getting the word out is just so *slick*.

Sexual and violent content exists in today's entertainment media for one reason only—because it sells. Ask a movie producer why he makes his movies, and he'll tell you—he's giving the public what it wants. Just like a car dealer. Or a shoe salesman. If this kind of content found no home in the marketplace, it would disappear.

---

61   Here are three examples:

From *For the Strength of Youth*, "Entertainment and Media": "Satan uses media to deceive you by making what is wrong and evil look normal, humorous, or exciting. He tries to mislead you into thinking that breaking God's commandments is acceptable and has no negative consequences for you or others."

From M. Russell Ballard, "Let Our Voices Be Heard," general conference, October 2003: "If we do not make good choices, the media can devastate our families and pull our children away. . . . Immorality and sexual innuendo are everywhere, causing some to believe that because everyone is doing it, it must be all right. . . . When you stop and think about it from a diabolically tactical point of view, fighting the family makes sense to Satan. When he wants to disrupt the work of the Lord . . . [he] attacks the family. [He] does so by attempting to disregard the law of chastity, to confuse gender, to desensitize violence . . . and to make immoral and deviant behavior seem like the rule rather than the exception."

From Gordon B. Hinckley, "Live up to Your Inheritance," general conference, October 1983: "The merchants of pornography and some designers of entertainment are as clever as hell itself with their beguiling wares."

62   The examples are everywhere—the drug trade, pornography, prostitution, exploitation of child labor, the alcohol and tobacco industry, and even the consummate time-wasting activities of mindless modern entertainment. All of these divert us from the Spirit and distract us from being anxiously engaged in a good cause (Doctrine and Covenants 58:27).

The fact that *you* don't spend time and money on violent or sexually oriented programming is of little consequence. You and I are the minority. There's a reason it's called mass media—it is designed for the masses. There's much more money to be made by creating entertainment for those living in the great and spacious building than those holding onto the iron rod (see 1 Nephi 8:26–27).

But the world of entertainment is not entirely what was once described as a vast wasteland.[63] Movies like *The Lion King* and *Frozen* have made Disney a great deal of money without explicit sexual and violent content.[64] Also, 2013's *God Is Not Dead* and 2014's *Son of God* and *Heaven Is for Real* are movies with straightforward, sympathetically portrayed Christian themes that all turned a profit at the box office, virtually guaranteeing that more movies like them will come in future years.[65]

And in the Church, movies such as *The Singles Ward* and *Charly* have ushered in the genre of LDS cinema, where Church-oriented comedies and dramas make regular appearances. In recent years, LDS filmmakers have sought wider audiences with the developing *Saints and Soldiers* film franchise and *The Saratov Approach*. Many of these film projects have been commercially successful.[66] Meanwhile, the LDS music and literary scenes are vibrant, with dozens of artists and authors on display at your local LDS bookstore.

---

63   The statement that television is a vast wasteland was made by former Federal Communications Commission (FCC) chairman Newton Minnow in May 1961: "When television is good . . . nothing is better. When television is bad, nothing is worse." He encouraged the people who ran television stations to spend a day actually watching the programs airing on their stations. He said, "I can assure you that what you will observe is a vast wasteland."

64   *The Lion King* cost an estimated $45 million to make in 1994. It has grossed just under $1 billion since then. *Frozen* cost $150 million to make in 2013, and at last count was sitting at $1.3 billion. *Frozen* is currently the fifth all-time grossing movie in history behind *Avatar*, *Titanic*, *The Avengers*, and the final Harry Potter movie. And *Frozen* is still going strong. (All figures from imdb.com.)

65   *Heaven Is for Real* cost $12 million and so far has grossed over $90 million in ticket sales (imdb.com).

66   *The Saratov Approach* is an independent film shot on a low budget. Nevertheless, in a limited release it has still grossed $2.1 million since October 2013. Meanwhile, *The Singles Ward* was released in February 2002 on a budget of a half-million dollars. By November it had grossed $1.2 million, a groundbreaking figure for a theatrical film targeting Mormons (imdb.com).

For years, producers of salacious programming have responded to viewer criticism with the same response: if you don't like it, don't watch. They are, of course, correct. If enough people don't watch, it *will* go away. But producers are also supremely safe in making the statement because they know the odds are high that the numbers of those who will watch highly sexual and violent content will vastly exceed the number of those who won't.

In this aspect of our lives, as with most others, the popular-culture disconnect between the Church and society as a whole is simply the result of where we stand. The river of filthy water (see 1 Nephi 12:16) will forever divide those who are holding fast to the iron rod from those in the great and spacious building who will forever mock us and freeze us out.

Well, if we are to be frozen out, so be it. The cold never bothered me anyway.

> **The short answer:** "In our Church we're taught that life is too short to fill our minds with junk. There's a lot of really bad behavior shown in movies and on TV that's presented as normal—but it's not or shouldn't be. I just don't choose to see it or listen to it. And there are a lot of other people like me."

## SCRIPTURE SUPPORT:

| | |
|---|---|
| Ephesians 6:11–17 | Put on the whole armor of God |
| Isaiah 52:11 | Touch no unclean thing; be ye clean that bear the vessels of the Lord |
| Article of Faith 1:13 | Seek after anything virtuous, lovely, of good report, or praiseworthy |

### Question #29: Dude, your parents really won't let you date until you're sixteen?

When I talk with young people about what questions most commonly come their way about the Church, this is number one. Perhaps it's a sign of how far apart we stand from the social mainstream that such a rule could be considered so unusual.

Personally, I don't know of any parents in the Church who object to the idea of restricting dating until sixteen, but I've encountered occasional resistance from some younger teenagers who see this line of demarcation as arbitrary and unnecessary for them individually due to their ahead-of-the-curve level of emotional maturity.

Speaking as the father of eleven, I appreciate that the Church doesn't spend much time defending or explaining its directive. The statement is simple: you should not date until you are sixteen years old. Parents understand that maturity is a work in progress for teenagers—a point usually lost on those in the middle of it.

But what parents sometimes forget is that while we are the ones who enforce the dating restriction, our children are the ones who must explain and defend it to their peers. In areas where LDS students are the majority (or at least a large minority), common awareness of the rule may minimize the difficulty, but in areas with a small LDS population, our children can feel backed into an uncomfortable and possibly even ostracism-worthy corner by their peers. This can be even more difficult if they themselves are not 100 percent convinced it's the right thing to do.

Let me speak directly to you, Mom and Dad. Despite all the social pressure to compromise, backing down on this is not only risky for your child but undermines the efforts of other parents in the ward and stake who will immediately be inundated with the news that "Brother and Sister Jones let Suzy go out on a date, and she's only fifteen."

If the Church's stance on dating is unpopular in your home, stand firm anyway. Too much is at risk for you to waffle on it. If your child is taking heat for it in school, invite them to take advantage of the time-honored parental tactic of blaming it on you or the Church.

It's better than caving in, but that's not the best solution. For a teen to blame the restriction on Mom, Dad, or the bishop undermines the gospel in the eyes of everyone who hears it—demonstrating, in their judgment, that the Church imposes unreasonable rules on members who are forced to comply. That's not the kind of seed any Church member wants to plant in a nonmember's heart. Far better is for teens to stand up in support of the gospel and simply state the rule along with their support of it.

If you're a teenager with a few doubts on this one, I can only say that while you may not be sixteen yet, you are old enough by now to have seen how the Lord has blessed your life when you obey the commandments. Think about that, and if you have to accept this particular commandment on faith, just do it. You can be like Nephi, who said to the angel, "I know that [God] loveth his children; nevertheless, I do not know the meaning of all things" (1 Nephi 11:17). When it comes to dating, in time you will understand. I promise.

> **The short answer:** "That's right. Our church recommends that teenagers don't start dating until we're sixteen. I don't have a problem with that."

## SCRIPTURE SUPPORT:

| | |
|---|---|
| Doctrine and Covenants 46:33 | Practice virtue and holiness continually |
| Doctrine and Covenants 88:40 | Wisdom receiveth wisdom; truth embraceth truth; virtue loveth virtue; light cleaveth unto light |

# QUESTIONS ABOUT
# THE THINGS WE DO

### *Question #30: Why don't you drink? Smoke? Do drugs?*

Thanks to all the health education we've received and our children receive today, everyone understands the risks of smoking as well as drinking and using illegal drugs. So the question here is really, "Why aren't you going along with the crowd?"

Answering with the old cliché, "Well if everyone jumped off a cliff, would you do it?" probably won't win many friends. Besides, it has the effect of belittling or antagonizing your friend. Neither will leave a positive impression. A simple, affirmative statement will enable you to declare your position as a disciple of Jesus Christ without running the risk of shaming your friend.

> **The Short Answer**: "Well, the main reason is that I don't want to. It's dangerous, it can become addictive, and it's obviously not good for you. In our church we believe our bodies are a gift from God and we need to stay away from that stuff. I'm sure you understand that."

Ending with the statement, "I'm sure you understand that," almost guarantees your friend will respond with a "Well, sure, I guess." But if not, remember your statement is respectful, clear, and, most importantly, correct. There is nothing in our stand to be ashamed of.

## SCRIPTURE SUPPORT:

Doctrine and Covenants 89     The Word of Wisdom

| 1 Corinthians 3:16–17 | Ye are the temple of God; if any man defile that temple, he shall be destroyed (The destruction mentioned could easily be the health effects of smoking, drugs, etc.) |
| 1 Corinthians 6:9–10 | Drunkenness identified as a trait of the unrighteous who will not inherit the kingdom of God |
| Ephesians 5:18 | Be not drunk with wine, but be filled with the Spirit |

### Question #31: Can you drink things like Coke and Mountain Dew?

If you are asked this question, then your friend probably already knows something about the Church and is aware of what, from a distance, can look confusing or even a little hypocritical.

For as long as I can remember, Church members have been explaining that the prohibition in the Word of Wisdom of tea and coffee is due to the caffeine they contain. We proudly explain that when the revelation was given in 1833, medical science was not aware of the inherent dangers of either tobacco or caffeine, so what looked illogical at the time was actually proof of the prophetic vision of Joseph Smith.

Well then, if caffeine is a no-no, doesn't it follow that you shouldn't be drinking caffeinated soft drinks? So why do you have a Diet Coke in your hand? Which, from their perspective, is a very fair question.

As we know, the Word of Wisdom as contained in section 89 of the Doctrine and Covenants does not mention caffeine. (After all, Joseph Smith received the revelation in 1833. Coca-Cola wasn't invented until 1886.) It only says that "hot drinks are not for the body" (Doctrine and Covenants 89:9). Church leaders long ago defined "hot drinks" as being tea and coffee. Even though caffeine is not directly mentioned in the revelation, through the years the Church has frequently warned members of its dangers.[67] Seen in this light, it may be easier to understand why there has been confusion on the subject from both inside and outside of the Church. Is caffeine banned or isn't it? If so, why does there seem to be so much hedging on the issue? If not, why does the Church keep talking about the evils of caffeine?

In my forty years in the Church, this has always been a touchy subject. I have heard members grouse that Brother So-and-So always has a Coke in his hand and then speculate on whether he is truly worthy of the temple recommend in his wallet. I've also heard—and I am not making this up—that there is a "secret ban" against caffeinated drinks and that "the Brethren can't really talk about it, but everyone knows it exists."

This issue came to a recent head in 2012 during the presidential campaign of Mitt Romney when an hour-long NBC news special on

---

67   See, for example, Clifford J. Stratton, "Caffeine—the Subtle Addiction," *Ensign*, June 1988, and Thomas J. Boud, MD, "The Energy Drink Epidemic," *Ensign*, December 2008.

the Church reported that Mormons don't drink caffeine. The story prompted the Church to restate its position that only tea and coffee, not caffeinated drinks in general, are banned for Church members. The Church's announcement received modest media coverage[68] and appears to have successfully quieted the debate for the time being.

And so, for any still in doubt, let me point out that with the exception of tea and coffee, the consumption of caffeinated drinks and even energy drinks is not prohibited by the Church. Discouraged perhaps, but not prohibited. This means you can hold your Monster in one hand and your temple recommend in the other if you wish. Do such drinks violate the spirit of the Word of Wisdom? And if they do, does it matter? Opinions differ. When it comes to proclaiming the word of the Lord, the Church reports. You decide.

> **The short answer:** "Yes, although there has been a lot of confusion about that through the years, even inside the Church. Almost from the beginning of the Church, we've been told not to drink tea or coffee. That rule still stands. But caffeinated drinks like Coke or Mountain Dew aren't officially banned. Of course, a lot of Church members choose not to drink caffeinated sodas or energy drinks. Others do. Life goes on."

## SCRIPTURE SUPPORT:

Doctrine and Covenants 89:7–9    Prohibition of strong drinks (alcohol), tobacco, and hot drinks

---

68    See Peggy Stack, "Mormon Caffeine Policy Clarified, Coke and Pepsi Officially OK for Latter-day Saints," *Salt Lake Tribune*, September 1, 2012.

**Question #32: *Why do you pay 10 percent of the money you make to your church?***

We believe The Church of Jesus Christ of Latter-day Saints is the restoration of Christ's original Church in its doctrine, power, and authority. One ancient principle restored by the Lord in modern times is the law of tithing, which states, in its totality, that members of the Church are to pay one-tenth of their increase to the Church.

That's it. No thousand-plus page tax code. No lengthy analysis. No legal precedents. The particulars of what constitutes your "increase" is between you and the Lord.

Paying tithing is good for two reasons—it blesses us, and it blesses the Church. Through it we discipline ourselves and our spending, while providing the Church with the means to build chapels, temples, and schools, and carry on the work of the Lord across the world. We believe that we are directly blessed by the Lord for paying tithing.

When people ask about tithing, it's often because they are intrigued, or baffled, about why we pay what seems such a large amount of money. When we say we are blessed for doing it, our answer can sound thin to our friends—especially if we can't answer the follow-up question, "How?"

Explaining the blessings of tithing presents the same difficulty as explaining how we receive inspiration and direction from the Holy Ghost. You can say the words, but if your friend has no real understanding of spiritual things, it's likely to be a difficult sell. As Elder Bednar has explained, the blessings of tithing are often subtle and can be difficult to express.[69] Regardless, we can always explain the principle of tithing and express our willingness to keep the Lord's commandment. Once again, a short answer really is the best.

> **The short answer:** "Paying a tenth of our earnings—or tithing—is one of the biblical principles restored to us in modern times. When we pay our tithing, we believe the Lord blesses us so that we barely miss it, if at all. For me, paying tithing has always been a privilege not an obligation."

---

69   See Elder David A. Bednar, "The Windows of Heaven," general conference, October 2013, for a discussion of the subtle blessings of tithing.

## SCRIPTURE SUPPORT:

| | |
|---|---|
| Genesis 14:20 | Abraham pays his tithing to Melchizedek |
| Malachi 3:10 | Bring the tithes to the storehouse, the windows of heaven will pour out a blessing |
| Doctrine and Covenants 119:3–6 | If we do not obey the law of tithing, we will not be worthy to dwell in Zion |

### Question #33: Why do young Mormons have to be missionaries?

Short of a picture of the Salt Lake Temple, no visual image immediately identifies the Church as well as the sight of two young elders in their white shirts and ties riding bicycles along the back streets and highways of the world. They and the sister missionaries who have now joined them in almost vast numbers are visible in nearly every country on earth. They are the pride and joy of the Church and an enduring object of curiosity for those not of our faith.

Parents of missionaries know that mentioning their son or daughter is away serving a Mormon mission is the best way possible to discuss the Church with a nonmember. Whether your friends are interested in the Church or not, everyone is interested in the missionaries and the level of dedication necessary for them to serve.

During the years when my children were serving missions, friends and acquaintances often asked a variation of the question, "Do they *have* to go on a mission?" It's an honest question. It's probably easier for someone not familiar with us to assume that there must be some compulsion involved in getting so many young men and women out the door. It then becomes our privilege to inform them that there is no compulsion, that these youth serve solely because they want to serve, and that they are even paying their own money for the right to do so.

Our young missionaries bless the world each day not only by the testimony of Jesus Christ they teach but by the sheer optimism they spread each day in the cities and countries in which they have been called to serve. The mere sight of them is a sermon, that in a world filled with slovenly self-absorption, there are still young men and women who can dedicate a portion of their lives to selflessly serving others. I've known many adults not of our faith who nevertheless cheer the missionaries on because in encouraging the missionaries they know they are encouraging a world where goodness, commitment, service, and virtue will survive.

**The short answer:** "They don't have to, but a large number of them do. They do it at their own expense because they want to serve the Lord. For them, and for the people they teach, it's an exciting, educational, and life-changing experience."

**SCRIPTURE SUPPORT:**

| | |
|---|---|
| Matthew 28:19–20 | The Lord gives the command to teach and baptize all nations |
| Doctrine and Covenants 4:3–4 | If ye have desires to serve God ye are called to the work; the field is white, all ready to harvest |

### Question #34: Why do you try to convert everyone? Why can't you let people just do their own thing?

I'm convinced that one of the reasons people don't ask us about the Church is because they're afraid of us—that once they ask us a question we'll never leave them alone, we'll turn them into a project, and we'll have the missionaries beating on their door day and night until they have to be rude to make us go away and leave them alone.

Their concerns are, of course, completely unfounded.

Naturally, none of us want to see ourselves in the description above. That's why I've written this book and hopefully why you're reading it—because we don't want to be the stereotyped pushy-project Mormons. When it comes to information about the Church, our friends deserve for us to be a resource, not a source of aggravation.

**The short answer:** "The Church helps me in spiritual ways and also in practical ways. If you find something that really works, I guess it's natural to want to share it with your friends. If people want to come and see what we're all about, we'd love to help them learn about what we have to offer in the Church. But if they don't want to learn about us, we leave them alone. We don't harass anyone."

### SCRIPTURE SUPPORT:

| | |
|---|---|
| 1 Peter 3:15 | Be ready always to give an answer to every man that asketh you |
| Alma 38:12 | Use boldness, but not overbearance that ye may be filled with love |

### *Question #35: Do you hoard food? Why?*

Many people find our efforts to store food to be curious, unusual, and perhaps strange.

To some it smacks of hoarding, and hoarding, by definition, is either for some questionable purpose or reflects a psychological impairment. It is our privilege to assure our friends that neither is the case. We are counseled to gather our food storage in a prudent and financially responsible way. For example, going into debt to store food is discouraged.[70]

We are also encouraged to produce as much of the food we store as possible. Church members have long been counseled to have gardens and preserve our little harvests.[71] The art of canning fruits and vegetables is alive and well in the Church even in urban wards and branches. Our goal is self-reliance and to have a year's supply of food, fuel, and money. We don't do this in anticipation of some imminent national or global social disruption or natural disaster. The many disruptions and disasters that can befall us in life are often far smaller in scale but still might make us glad for the food and fuel we've stored—for example, the loss of a job or the long-term effects of illness or injury.

Because of our desire to live providently and independently, several companies have sprung up over the years that actively market food storage products to Mormons. I've watched with good humor as Church members from other parts of the world visit the Mormon corridor of Idaho, Utah, and Arizona and are astounded to see a wide variety of food storage items on the shelves of Walmart and similar stores. Members

---

70   See, for example Ezra Taft Benson, "Prepare for the Days of Tribulation," general conference, October 1980: "Members of the Church have been counseled to be thrifty and self-reliant; to avoid debt, pay tithes and a generous fast offering; be industrious; and have sufficient food, clothing, and fuel on hand to last at least one year."

71   See, for one of many examples, Spencer W. Kimball, "The Time to Labor Is Now," general conference, October 1975: "In previous times we have urged you to plant gardens and trees. We congratulate you on the number of gardens this year. Everywhere we drive, from city to city, we see gardens that were not there before. Rows of corn, red tomato plants, carrots, onions, radishes, squash, and other plants. We congratulate you! We see ward gardens and community gardens and neighborhood gardens. We are sure that you have reduced, to some extent, the high cost of living by having these fresh vegetables from your own gardens."

living in areas where there is not a significant LDS population can still order food storage products by mail.

In all of this, we seek to follow the call of modern prophets who, from the founding of the Church to the present day, have invited Church members to strive for self-sufficiency. This has never been done in a spirit of panic or gloom but rather as an act of faith and in anticipation of the personal growth that comes from knowing you are prepared to the fullest extent possible for life's inevitable challenges.

Recently, though, I've seen a new and darker wrinkle in food storage marketing to the wider population—which may create a false perception among the uninformed. Some companies are now suggesting that the government itself is secretly hoarding food, which marketers imply will result in less food available for the rest of us. As a result, food storage is now sometimes marketed as an act of patriotism, and information about food storage constitutes "what the government [or FEMA] doesn't want you to know."[72] In 2011, the Internet flashed with the so-called news that government agents had raided a "Mormon food storage facility in Tennessee" (apparently a cannery in Nashville or Knoxville), demanding a list of clients, allegedly for the purpose of confiscating their food supply. Glowering blogs predicted that the "government was now treating prepared patriots as terrorists."[73] Ultimately the story was proved to be false but probably not before instigating the sale of additional crates of food storage by those who exploit fear and paranoia for financial gain.

The two questions I am most commonly asked in connection with my family's admittedly incomplete food storage effort are, "Do Mormons believe in some about-to-arrive social or political Armageddon?" and, "In the event of a food shortage, will you share?"

No, we don't. And (speaking for my wife and me), yes, we will.

---

72  The idea that there may be secret government plans to hoard food and keep it from "hard-working Americans" has been used in the sales pitch of Food4Patriots. com. See http://secure.food4patriots.com/letter/index.php.

73  From www.naturalnews.com. Another example from their site quotes a group called Oath Keepers with the following: "The government might be trying to gather intelligence on food-storing Americans in order to later come and confiscate that food, or worse—after all, freedom-loving patriots who are preparing for social upheaval are a threat to the power structure that seeks to tighten the noose of tyranny around the neck of society."

As Church members, we believe Paul's words that "in the last days perilous times shall come" (2 Timothy 3:1). Since Paul's words were written, we have seen no shortage of perilous times in the world, fueled by war and natural disaster. We are confident that we have not seen the last of any of these kinds of events nor will we until the Second Coming of Jesus Christ. But we claim no secret timetable for that glorious event or for the great Armageddon that will precede it. Instead we try to live providently and faithfully, recognizing that life brings challenges, large and small, to us all.

As for sharing our food storage with others—we already do. My good wife, who is so often more in tune with the Spirit than I, has frequently delivered care packages from our food storage to members and nonmember friends who are struggling in their own lives. I'm glad to hear about it when she does. What does it mean to be a disciple of Jesus Christ if not to share our time, talents, and substance with those truly in need?[74]

> **The short answer:** "We don't hoard food, but we do believe in being self-reliant. For the last fifty years or so, we've been encouraged to store a year's worth of food and basic supplies. You just never know, right?"

## SCRIPTURE SUPPORT:

| | |
|---|---|
| Doctrine and Covenants 1:12 | Prepare for that which is to come |
| Doctrine and Covenants 38:30 | If ye are prepared ye shall not fear |
| Doctrine and Covenants 88:119 | Prepare every needful thing |

---

74   So many scriptures to pick from. Here are a few: Proverbs 19:17, "He that hath pity upon the poor lendeth unto the Lord." Matthew 10:8, "Freely ye have received, freely give." Matthew 25:35, "I was an hungred, and ye gave me meat." Mosiah 4:16, "Administer of your substance unto him that standeth in need."

### Question #36: In America, aren't Mormons all Republicans? Doesn't that make your faith unwelcoming to those who don't support the Republican political agenda?

In 2012, Mitt Romney ran for the US presidency. He was, of course, a member of The Church of Jesus Christ of Latter-day Saints. Not surprisingly, he carried the majority of the Mormon vote in November in what was a losing effort against the incumbent president.

The Church is known throughout the world as a morally conservative church, and in the United States, the party of mainstream conservatism is the Republican Party. In a 2012 research project from the Pew Research Center, 75 percent of American Mormons identified themselves as Republican or leaning Republican.[75] But despite those overwhelming numbers, the Church aggressively cultivates a stance of strict neutrality on political races. The Church never endorses any candidate—even Mitt. It has even released an official statement of political neutrality.[76]

This does not stop the Church, however, from occasionally getting involved in ballot measures involving what it considers to be important moral issues. The Church sees a difference between political issues and moral issues—typically ballot questions and amendments—that impact public policy.

An example of this came in 2008, when California voters were asked to decide whether the California Supreme Court's decision legalizing same-sex marriage should be reversed with an amendment to the state constitution defining marriage as solely between one man and one woman. The Church has consistently opposed same-sex marriage (see Question #25 for a discussion on why), and Church leaders came out in support of Proposition 8. Prominent Mormons donated large amounts of money (roughly $20 million) to fund the campaign to repeal the California court's decision, and the Church encouraged

---

75   See the Pew Research Center, pewforum.org, "Mormons in America—Certain in Their Beliefs, Uncertain of Their Place in Society," January 12, 2012.

76   You can read the Church's official statement of political neutrality at www. mormonnewsroom.org. Search *political neutrality*.

California Mormons to organize and get Prop 8 passed.[77] The measure was approved in a close 52 to 48 percent vote. Over 13 million votes were cast—a voter turnout rate of over 70 percent. Mormon money and support were credited by both sides as the crucial factor in the vote—to the cheers of supporters and the anger of those who opposed. Throughout the divisive campaign, the Church insisted it was not anti-gay, just pro-marriage, and was simply exercising its democratic right to speak out on moral issues.[78]

This type of Church involvement in the political process does not happen often. Since 2008 the Church has been largely silent politically even when it had the chance to endorse one of its own in the battle for the presidency. Instead, the Church merely reminds voters to learn about the issues and then vote their conscience.

The Church's official statement of political neutrality says in part,

> The Church's mission is to preach the gospel of Jesus Christ, not to elect politicians. [It] is neutral in matters of party politics. . . .
>
> The Church does not endorse, promote or oppose political parties, candidates or platforms . . . [or] attempt to direct its members as to which candidate or party they should give their votes to. This policy applies whether or not a candidate for office is a member of The Church of Jesus Christ of Latter-day Saints.[79]

In releasing the statement to the news media, Church spokesperson Scott Trotter said the Church stresses that "good can be found in all the platforms of various political parties."[80]

To its credit, the Church has gone to lengths to make its Sunday worship meetings political-free zones, discouraging people from advocating partisan political agendas in sacrament meeting talks, fast and

---

77   See Jesse McKinley and Kirk Johnson, "Mormons Tipped Scale in Ban on Gay Marriage," *New York Times*, November 14, 2008. The article quotes California's Project Marriage saying that half of the $40 million raised to support Prop 8 came from Mormon donations.

78   Ibid.

79   From the Church's statement on political neutrality. See footnote 91.

80   See Matt Canham and Thomas Burr, "Top Mormon Church Posts Dominated by Registered Republicans," *Salt Lake Tribune*, December 6, 2012.

testimony meetings, and classroom instruction. Teachers are instructed not to let classes devolve into political discussions but to keep the focus squarely on the gospel of Jesus Christ.[81]

So the answer to this question is that, yes, in the United States The Church of Jesus Christ of Latter-day Saints is overwhelmingly Republican, but, no, the faith welcomes everyone, regardless of their political views. That is the policy of the Church, but it's up to us, the members, to make sure it's true.

> **The short answer:** "In a national poll, about 3 out of 4 Mormons identified themselves as Republicans. The Church itself, however, is strictly neutral on political issues, although occasionally the Church leadership will speak out on what it feels are important *moral* issues."

## SCRIPTURE SUPPORT:

| | |
|---|---|
| Mark 12:13–17 | Jesus makes clear his role as Savior and teacher of gospel truths and does not allow himself to become an advocate for partisan politics |
| Alma 4:15–19 | Alma the Younger resigns his political position so he can solely concentrate on his ministry |

---

81 See "Keeping the Doctrine Pure," chapter 11 in *Teaching: No Greater Call*. Teachers are admonished to teach with the scriptures and words of the modern prophets while using only Church-produced teaching materials. Specifically, teachers are told to avoid speculation, misquoting, gospel hobbies, sensational stories, reshaping Church history, private interpretations, and unorthodox views. If lesson manuals are followed closely and the teacher directs the conversation from any of the problem areas listed above, political issues will never become classroom issues.

# QUESTIONS ABOUT THE TEMPLE

***Question #37: What's the difference between a temple and a regular Mormon church?***

In my opinion, the greatest difficulty we have in adequately explaining the role of the temple in our lives is that our general society has lost a collective sense of what it means to be in the presence of something sacred. In the absence of a sense of the sacred, holy sites of churches of all faiths are just buildings or hills or groves of trees—perhaps interesting to look at but not worthy of any special sense of reverence or refined conduct. As a result, I have seen people enter some of the beautiful religious buildings of the world with noisy, disrespectful attitudes. They snap pictures while laughing and conversing loudly, even when others around them may be deep in prayer or contemplation.

Without an understanding of what it means to be in a holy place and the respect due to such places, even if they do not resonate with your own religious faith, it will be an uphill battle to convey the reverential gratitude we feel to be in the presence of, or even to discuss, the holy temple—the House of the Lord.

It will help to use words and phrases like *sacred, set apart, a place where the Spirit of the Lord can be found, a place of quiet reverence, a place where we can put things in proper perspective, a place where we can set aside our problems and draw close to God, a place where we can receive inspiration and revelation.* All of these may help your friend to understand the sacred nature of the temple, but we must also realize that your friend may need to first understand the idea of something as being sacred and worthy of our highest respect, reverence, and level of preparation to attend, specifically in regards to our dress and conduct. This idea may be new to your friend, even if he attends another church. In many modern churches, attendees come as they would to see a popular movie or music concert. Their dress is casual, and their expectation is to be entertained as much as enlightened. They know that churches—even churches within their own denomination—are competing for their support, and many like the idea that they may dictate the terms under which they will deign to approach God.

So when we attempt to answer the simple question of "What's the difference between a temple and a regular Church building?" we should give a thoughtful answer, recognizing that your friend may still have only a little understanding of what the words mean.

> **The short answer:** "Churches are where we meet each Sunday to sing, pray, worship, and receive the sacrament. A temple is a dedicated House of the Lord. It is a 'higher' place where we can feel His presence more completely. It's where we make sacred covenants with God."

## SCRIPTURE SUPPORT:

| | |
|---|---|
| Isaiah 2:2–3 | The Lord's house shall be established in the top of the mountains . . . and all nations shall flow unto it |
| Habakkuk 2:20 | The Lord is in his holy temple |

### Question #38: *What do you do inside temples?*

The work of temples is sacred, not secret. We can speak in the broadest generalities about what occurs inside sacred temple walls but little beyond that.

What do we do inside temples? We draw closer to God, our Eternal Father, and His Son, Jesus Christ. We learn more about Them and Their ways than in any other place on earth. We make sacred covenants that bind us to God, and He to us, for eternity. And in temples we are also bound to each other as eternal families, secure and happy in the knowledge that our most cherished and loving relationships will extend beyond life to the eternities to come.

What do we do inside temples? We are given the *knowledge* we will need to be able to one day return to His presence and the *power* to do so.

> **The short answer:** "A temple is a dedicated House of the Lord where we make sacred covenants with God and where sacred ordinances needed for eternal life are performed—such as marriage sealings, not just for time but for all eternity, and baptisms for those who have died without a knowledge of Jesus Christ."

## SCRIPTURE SUPPORT:

Doctrine and Covenants 6:12　　Trifle not with sacred things

Doctrine and Covenants 109:13　　All people who enter the Lord's house may feel His power; it is a place of holiness

## Question #39: Why do you get baptized for dead people?

When I was young, I was a geek. Unfortunately, it was a long time before geeks were cool. Not that I was a techno-kid. I was someone who spent time thinking deeply about stuff nobody else did. I would talk to friends about my ponderings, and they would look at me like I had just flown in from a distant planet.

"Who thinks about this stuff?" they would ask.

Silly me. I thought everybody did.

Here's one of the things I thought about in the days before I joined the Church: There are a lot of different churches around the world—Christianity, Judaism, Hinduism, Islam, Taoism, etc. They can't all be right. There has to be a central truth to the matter. God had to be *something*—a Christian, a Hindu—whatever. But let's say, God was a Christian. Christians are big on baptism. A lot of churches believe that if you aren't baptized, you're going to hell. *So what happens*, I wondered, *to some kid born in second-century China who died when he was ten and never heard of Jesus Christ in his entire life? Is he going to hell?* I was no teenage theologian, but I figured it didn't take Einstein to know that wouldn't be fair.

Odd as it may sound, this question was a major impediment to my ever seriously considering joining a Christian church. And when my wife and I took the missionary discussions, I expected my question about the second-century kid from China to stop the missionaries cold.

But it didn't.

Instead, in about ninety seconds they gave me the only plausible answer I have ever found to the question that I'd thought about for years. And forty years later (at this writing), I am still happily in the Church.

The doctrine of baptism for the dead, as practiced in The Church of Jesus Christ of Latter-day Saints, is both simple and elegant. It extends the mercy of Christ's Atonement to all, without violating the justice that requires all essential ordinances to be performed on the pathway to exaltation. It is both logical and beautiful. It opens the mortal mind to an expanded view of the eternities unknown to the rest of the world. It is mighty and marvelous, touching and tender. It is service at its most sacred. The world would be lost without it.

Each time I've been asked about baptism for the dead, I have always felt it a privilege to respond.

**The short answer:** "In the temple we baptize living people on behalf of those who have died without receiving the gospel. After all, Jesus said that everyone must be baptized. What happens to all the people in the world who died without that chance—or who lived their lives without ever having heard of Jesus Christ?"

## SCRIPTURE SUPPORT:

| | |
|---|---|
| John 3:5 | Without baptism one cannot enter into the kingdom of God |
| Matthew 3:13–17 | Christ is baptized to fulfill all righteousness |
| 1 Corinthians 15:29 | If the dead rise not at all, why are they baptized for the dead? |

## Question #40: What do you mean by being "sealed" to your spouse?

Celestial marriage is the crowning ordinance of the gospel.[82]

In a world of no-fault divorce, where marriage is widely considered to exist primarily for the personal satisfaction of each partner, the idea of temple marriage is seen sometimes as an antiquated fantasy or as pie-in-the-sky optimism. The fact that millions find joy and fulfillment in their temple marriage is often overlooked in the cynical world view that wraps modern society.

In older times, the value of marriage as a partnership and merging of souls was understood, which made the concept of eternal marriage a far easier philosophic sell. Today marriage itself is viewed with skepticism, making the idea of an eternal union seem of doubtful value.

Nevertheless, the Church pushes on. Our rates of overall mental and physical health, and family and emotional stability exceed the nation as a whole by every measure,[83] but our view of the eternal nature of marriage and family struggles to gain a foothold in our use-it-and-toss-it commercial culture.

I mention this to point out another disconnect between Church members and society at large that we often overlook. The idea of a temple sealing that binds our spouse and children to us forever by virtue of the holy priesthood may seem like a no-brainer benefit of being a member of the Church, but our friends may view the concept warily. It may sound more like a potentially messy encumbrance to be avoided than a blessed union of souls. When we discuss the value of temple marriage, we may have to spend more time than we'd expect having to discuss the value of marriage itself—even sometimes to our married friends.

For now, a simple explanation of temple marriage remains the best way to proceed. Like all gospel seeds, it is always wise to plant and then leave the harvest to the Lord.

---

82    Bruce R. McConkie, Conference Report, April 1970, 27.

83    Studies abound on this topic. Here are just a few summaries. For physical health see Matea Gold, "Mormons among Nation's Healthiest, Researchers Say," *Los Angeles Times*, April 16, 1977, and Mark W. Cannon and Danielle Stockton, "UCLA Study Shows Mormons Live Longer," *Deseret News*, April 13, 2010. For mental health studies, see Allen E. Bergin and Marie Cornwall, "Religion and Mental Health: Mormons and Other Groups," Annual meeting of the Society for the Scientific Study of Religion, Salt Lake City, 1989.

**The short answer:** "We believe that in our temples we can be married for eternity and not just until 'death do us part' and that our children can be ours eternally as well. We call this being 'sealed.' It is a great blessing. It helps us live together in harmony and keeps us focused as a family on Jesus Christ, who makes it all possible."

## SCRIPTURE SUPPORT:

| | |
|---|---|
| 1 Corinthians 11:11 | Neither is the man without the woman, neither the woman without the man, in the Lord |
| Doctrine and Covenants 132:19–20 | The glory men and women will inherit when they are sealed by the priesthood in the covenant of eternal marriage (the entire section deals with the subject) |

## Question #41: My wife and I already believe we're married forever. You're telling me we're not?

If this question comes up for you, as it has for me, it will be a tender moment. The truth is that if we say to our friends that the standard marriage ceremony remains in force only until death separates them, they will usually tell us we are wrong. They believe sincerely that their marriage will continue after death and that the phrase "until death do you part" is (1) a solemn promise that they will cleave only to each other for the rest of their mortal lives, and (2) simply acknowledging that they will be parted for a time when one of the spouses dies and the other continues to live. When we use the words of their marriage vow against them in a way that they believe misstates the meaning, they are not likely to respond positively. They will perceive us as telling them what they believe, and they won't like it any more than we do when people do the same thing to us.

As a result, I would never use the "death do you part" phrase in a discussion of this topic. Insisting that our interpretation of the phrase is the only correct one is insulting. Rather, I would just state what we believe.

**The short answer:** "I promise I'm not 'telling' you anything, but we believe that the power to seal on earth and have it be sealed in heaven can only be performed by someone with the authority to administer that ordinance. And we believe that that priesthood authority exists uniquely in The Church of Jesus Christ of Latter-day Saints."

## SCRIPTURE SUPPORT:

| | |
|---|---|
| Matthew 16:18–19 | And whatsoever thou shalt bind on earth shall be bound in heaven |
| Doctrine and Covenants 132 | The entire section deals with the sealing ordinance and makes the case for the need for priesthood authority in performing it |

**ADDITIONAL SUPPORT:**

A friend of mine once said she responded to this question in a different way—pointing out that the Lord has great respect for the holy union of souls we call marriage, including those marriages performed outside the Mormon Church, which constitute about 99 percent of the marriages performed in the world today. But because the sealing power is so important, He has commanded us as a Church to devote a huge amount of time, energy, and financial resources into seeking out our ancestors so that their marriages—like ours—can be sealed for time and eternity. These proxy weddings are performed by the thousands every week in the temples by those who hold the sacred priesthood authority. These after-the-fact sealings are a gift and reward from a loving Heavenly Father to all those who have lived their lives in a state of matrimony, quietly serving God and each other. Our role in researching our family history and taking part in these sacred ordinances is our humble effort to do the same thing—to serve God and each other.

Your friend may not agree, but at least if this issue concerns him, then he is someone committed to the idea of marriage, which puts him ahead of many people in today's world. Compliment him on his marriage and its success and move on.

### Question #42: Can I go see what a temple looks like on the inside? Why not?

Temples are beautiful. They're beautiful for their architecture. Many are unique, yet all seem to give a glimpse of heaven just by their appearance.

They're beautiful for the spirit they radiate. People enjoy just seeing a temple or being near one. As a result, it's natural to want to go inside.

So we'll begin with the short answer first.

> **The short answer:** "Because what goes on in the temple is so sacred, only members of the Church who are committed to keeping God's commandments are allowed to go inside. However, all new temples are open to the public before they are dedicated, and you can see pictures of the interiors of several temples. Would you like to take a look?"

There are a few pictures of temple interiors on lds.org, but you have to know where to find them. At lds.org, click Resources—Temples—Why We Build Temples—Inside the Temple. On that page are four beautiful interior shots of temples with an accompanying article.

Or you can visit the Church Distribution Center at store.lds.org and order *Temples of The Church of Jesus Christ of Latter-day Saints,* a beautiful but inexpensive magazine-style booklet filled with articles and pictures of temples interiors and exteriors. You'll find it under Magazines—Special Issues. You might want to order more than one so you will have them instantly available to give to friends.

By being able to immediately show your friend what temples look like on the inside, you will be able to deflect the idea of the temple as a secret place where mysterious things happen. Instead, he will be able to see and feel that temples are as beautiful on the inside as the outside.

Additionally, if there is a temple under construction in your area, you might want to check and see if dates have been scheduled for an open house. If so, you will likely hear about it in your Sunday meetings, but you can also check on the Church calendar of upcoming events at lds.org/church/events.

### SCRIPTURE SUPPORT:

| | |
|---|---|
| Psalm 24:3–4 | Who shall ascend into the hill of the Lord? . . . He that hath clean hands and a pure heart |

## Question #43: What about the funny underwear Mormons wear?

In our increasing secular and hardened world, our sacred temple garments have regrettably become the butt of jokes and late-night comedy monologues. People who make such comments unwittingly become the modern embodiment of those in Lehi's dream who stand "in the attitude of mocking and pointing their fingers towards those who had come at and were partaking of the fruit" (1 Nephi 8:27).

It's my experience that people who ask us about our garments literally have no idea what they're talking about, and it is not difficult for them to give offense without realizing it. Despite the pain we feel when we see the things of God mocked so casually, we would do well to remember what the Savior said on the cross: "Father, forgive them; for they know not what they do" (Luke 23:34). It is then our privilege to lift, however slightly, their view with our answer.

Instead of one short answer, here are three. I hope that one will work for you.

> **Short answer 1**: "Well, even though I know you don't mean to give offense, what seems funny to you is actually sacred to us. Temple garments, as we call them, are simple, white underclothing, usually in two pieces like a T-shirt top and shorts. We wear them to remind us of the commitment we've made to do our best to be disciples of Jesus Christ."

> **Short answer 2**: "They are simple, white underclothing, usually in two pieces like a T-shirt top and shorts. We wear them as an outward expression of an inner commitment to follow the Savior."

> **Short answer 3**: "Have you ever seen someone wearing a clerical collar? What does it symbolize? So a clerical collar is a visible symbol that the person is a minister—a disciple of Christ. Now, what does a wedding ring symbolize? So a wedding ring is a visible symbol that you are married and devoted solely to your husband or wife. So just like a clerical collar or a wedding ring, temple garments are something we wear that are a symbol and a personal reminder of our desire to follow Christ."

## SCRIPTURE SUPPORT:

| | |
|---|---|
| Isaiah 52:1 | Awake, O Zion, and put on thy beautiful garments |
| Revelation 16:15 | Blessed is he that keepeth his garments |

## ADDITIONAL SUPPORT:

In 2014 the Church released a video that explains the role of special clothing worn by members of various religious faiths throughout the world, including those worn by members of the Church. It displays temple garments and temple robes in a respectful and reverent manner. You can find it at lds.org. Search for *temple garment video*. It is a powerful resource for you to share. Hopefully, you will watch it with the person asking the question instead of just inviting him to watch it himself.

## Question #44: Why do you have a picture of the temple in your room/ house?

Of course, you will only be asked this question if you *do* have a picture of the temple in your room or house. We have been counseled to have pictures of the temple in our homes as a reminder of the eternal nature of families and as an additional source of the peace that should prevail there.[84]

Separate from the personal spiritual blessings of having a picture of the temple in our home, its prominent place on a living room or bedroom wall can draw questions from our friends. As always, we will do best when we keep our answers short. Asking why we have a picture of a temple is not an open invitation to discuss the doctrine of temple worship, marriage sealings, baptism for the dead, personal worthiness, etc. Give a short answer, and if your friend feels impressed to ask a second question, he will.

**The short answer:** "Seeing a picture of the temple reminds me to try and be a disciple of Jesus Christ. It makes me want to be closer to Him. And besides, it's a beautiful building, isn't it?"

## SCRIPTURE SUPPORT:

Articles of Faith 1:13      Seek after anything virtuous, lovely, of good report, or praiseworthy

---

84  See, for example, Thomas S. Monson, "The Holy Temple—A Beacon to the World," general conference, April 2011, quoting President Spencer W. Kimball: "It would be a fine thing if . . . parents would have in every bedroom in their house a picture of the temple so [their children] from the time [they are] infant[s] could look at the picture every day [until] it becomes a part of [their lives]" (brackets in original).

# QUESTIONS ABOUT
# THE BOOK OF MORMON

### Question #45: What is the Book of Mormon?

I have been asked this question more than once from people encountering the Book of Mormon for the first time. It's my experience that most people have heard of it but few know anything about it. What *is* this thing, they ask. And they have good reason to ask—it's not like any other book on earth.

The Book of Mormon is a compilation of the writing of many prophets, yet it comes to us from only one—Joseph Smith. This alone makes it unique among all scripture. It makes bold claims. Could anything be bolder than the story of Christ's personal visit to the Western Hemisphere after His Resurrection? Its stories and sermons teach spiritual concepts of both astounding depth with unrivaled simplicity. Consider all we have from the Book of Mormon that brings us closer to God:

- Lehi's dream (see 1 Nephi 8).
- "I will go and do the things the Lord has commanded" (1 Nephi 3:7).
- "Men are that they might have joy" (2 Nephi 2:25).
- The hard-won testimony of Enos (see Enos 1:1–6).
- King Benjamin's discourse: "Are we not all beggars?" (see Mosiah 2–4, specifically Mosiah 4:19).
- Abinadi's testimony to King Noah (see Mosiah 12–13).
- Alma baptizes at the Waters of Mormon, inviting followers "to stand as a witness of God in all times and in all things" (Mosiah 18:9 [8–11]).
- Alma the Younger and the four sons of Mosiah are converted by an angel (see Mosiah 27:8–17).
- The missionary experiences of Alma and Amulek (see Alma 8–16).

- King Lamoni prays: "I will give away all my sins to know thee" (Alma 22:18).
- Korihor, the anti-Christ (see Alma 30).
- Alma's counsel to each of his sons (see Alma 36–42).
- Captain Moroni and the title of liberty (see Alma 46).
- Samuel the Lamanite testifies Christ shall come (see Helaman 13–15).
- The day and a night and a day as if it was one day (see 3 Nephi 1).
- Christ comes to the Americas, establishes His Church, and initiates a four-hundred-year period of peace and prosperity (see 3 Nephi 11–28).
- The chronicle of the fall of the Nephites (see Mormon 1–5).
- The Brother of Jared sees the Lord (see Ether 3).
- Mormon's epistle on baptism for children (see Moroni 8:8–14).
- Moroni seals the record of the Nephites by inviting everyone to pray to know if the record is true, for "by the power of the Holy Ghost ye may know the truth of all things" (Moroni 10:3–5).

This is hardly a complete list of the dramatic stories, powerful sermons, and revealed doctrine contained in the Book of Mormon. Its power to change lives is unequalled. As Joseph Smith said, "I told the brethren that . . . a man would get nearer to God by abiding by its precepts than by any other book" (title page of the Book of Mormon).

> **The short answer**: "The Book of Mormon came from prophets of God who lived in the Americas, just as the Holy Bible came from prophets who lived in the Holy Land. We believe Joseph Smith translated it from the original ancient writings through the power of God just before the Church was founded in 1830. Would you like a copy to read?"

## SCRIPTURE SUPPORT:

| | |
|---|---|
| John 10:16 | Other sheep I have, which are not of this fold |
| Ezekiel 37:16–19 | The Lord will take the stick of Judah (the Bible) and the stick of Joseph (the Book of Mormon) and make them one |

### Question #46: Didn't Joseph Smith really just make up the Book of Mormon and write it himself?

The time it took for Joseph Smith to get from "I, Nephi, having been born of goodly parents" to "the Eternal Judge of both quick and dead. Amen"[85] was basically three months. The stories told of Joseph during the translation process give no hint of revision or review. Joseph talked only slowly enough for his words to be copied down, sentence after sentence, page after page after page.[86]

What kind of knowledge and imagination would it take for someone to create the Book of Mormon? Here is a brief list adapted from a tongue-in-cheek assignment given by BYU professor Hugh Nibley to students studying the Book of Mormon:

- You must be twenty-three years old without any formal education past what we would now consider to be the seventh-grade level.
- Describe in detail a people and history of which you had no formal knowledge. Describe their manners, customs, arts, industries, and political and religious institutions.
- Use literary and stylistic writing forms unknown to you but consistent with writing styles used in Middle Eastern cultures.[87]
- Create a story covering a thousand years, utilizing more than one hundred original names while keeping several interrelated local histories going at once.

---

85  1 Nephi 1:1 and Moroni 10:34, the beginning of the first verse and end of the last verse of the Book of Mormon.

86  Oliver Cowdery, who acted as scribe for Joseph Smith during the translation process more than any other, described the translation process as follows: "These were days never to be forgotten; to sit under the sound of a voice dictated by the inspiration of heaven . . . as he translated with the Urim and Thummim, or as the Nephites would have said, 'interpreters,' the history or record called 'The Book of Mormon.'" Letter from Oliver Cowdery to W. W. Phelps (Letter 1), September 7, 1834. Published in *Latter Day Saints' Messenger and Advocate*, vol. 1, no. 1. Kirtland, Ohio, October 1834.

87  In 1969, an LDS researcher named John Welch noticed evidence in the Book of Mormon of a phrase and sentence-construction technique often found in Semitic languages called *chiasmus*. He suggested this was an evidence that Joseph Smith could not have written the book by himself. Linguistic analysis of the Book of Mormon is a broad subject. A brief (but thoroughly sourced) overview of the subject of linguistics can be found on Wikipedia.org in an article entitled "Linguistics and the Book of Mormon."

- Create multiple religious sermons of astonishing depth and spirituality.
- Nothing in the book can contradict itself, either doctrinally or historically.
- Nothing except minor punctuation and spelling can be corrected once it falls from your lips or pen. Your first draft is also your final product.
- You have three months to get virtually all of it done. Good luck.[88]

This little exercise will, of course, impress no one but the already converted. We will convince no one of the truthfulness of the Book of Mormon by an appeal to logic, reason, or evidence. We can offer all the reasons in the world why Joseph could not have written the Book of Mormon by himself, and it will make no difference. The things of God simply cannot be discerned by a mind that either won't or can't perceive a universe of spiritual truth (1 Corinthians 2:14). One who relies only on the logic of the sciences to prove every truth inevitably misses the point of spiritual things. Like the unbelieving Nephites discounting and arguing against the signs of the birth of Jesus, one may say, "It is not reasonable that there should be a Christ" (see Helaman 16:15–18).

You can still use logic to answer this question—just recognize that you aren't likely to be successful. Regardless, if asked, I will still point out that logical minds should be able to conclude that the complexity of structure, character, and depth of doctrine contained in the Book of Mormon would be an astounding writing accomplishment for the most practiced author, let alone an essentially unschooled twenty-three-year-old who had never written anything of substance in his life. But I have yet to meet anyone who accepts the Book of Mormon as scripture because of its dense plot and structural complexity. We rise and fall on our testimony, as does the book itself.

**The short answer:** "That would be a tall order for a twenty-three-year-old man with almost no formal education. There have always been critics who make the claim that Joseph Smith just wrote it, but the only real way to judge the Book of Mormon is to read it yourself. I've read it, and just like millions of others, I've found that just like the Holy Bible

---

88 Adapted from "The Book of Mormon Challenge," *The Collected Works of Hugh Nibley*, col. 8, ch. 11, pp. 221–222.

it contains the word of God and the gospel of Jesus Christ.
Would you like a copy to read?"

## SCRIPTURE SUPPORT:

| | |
|---|---|
| Luke 24:32 | The Apostles' hearts burned while Christ opened the scriptures to them (the power of the Holy Ghost to convey truth) |
| Moroni 10:3–5 | By the power of the Holy Ghost ye shall know the truth of all things |

***Question #47: The story of how the Book of Mormon was written—
with angels and gold plates that conveniently no longer exist—is just
too much. How can you believe a story like that?***

Not only have I run into this question through the years, I've asked
it.

It was when my wife and I were being taught by the missionaries.
I was looking for reasons to doubt and was having a hard time finding
any—until this part of the story came along.

"So," said Elder Ipsen, "Joseph Smith translated the Book of
Mormon from the gold plates given to him by the Angel Moroni."

This was exciting news to me. My doubting mind instantly locked
on something to believe: the original plates—they existed. Translation
could be verified. "So where are the plates now?" I asked, really excited
for the first time during the discussion.

The briefest pause. "Well, the angel took them back."

I said very slowly, "Riiight . . ." I'm not sure either the elders or my
wife knew it, but we were rapidly approaching the breaking point in my
willingness to continue the missionary discussions. I was not willing to
accept a you-just-have-to-believe-it answer. I'd heard that one too many
times from the other churches I had investigated.

But it's times like these that the angels insert themselves into our
lives and give stumbling mortals a push in the right direction. Elder
Ipsen paused and then with confidence offered, "But don't take our word
for it."

A pause. "Okay. Why not?"

"Because we could be lying."

Another pause. It was certainly a novel concept. Safe to say he had
my attention.

"Listen," he continued, "we're missionaries for our Church. What do
you expect us to say? That this is all false? Of course not. You won't find
out if anything we say is true just by listening to us. There's only one way
to know for sure."

"And what's that?"

He pulled out his scriptures and turned to the back of the Book of
Mormon. "Would you read for us these verses from Moroni chapter 10?"

That's how I was introduced to the concept of asking in faith, with
real intent, and receiving revelation from the Holy Ghost in answer to
my questions. As I read it, I could feel my world expanding.

"If you do this," Elder Ipsen said with a big smile on his face, "we won't lose your business."

The trick to all of this—as I would discover—was the asking with real intent. It's obvious and simplistic to say that you can't fake sincerity, but over the years I've seen struggling converts attempt to do just that in their approach to God—as if a moment's earnestness is enough to bring down the powers of heaven. But casual prayers that muster up only a vague rumble of inner feelings aren't enough. It was two or three months after the elders challenged me to discover the truth for myself that events conspired in my life to finally bring me to the point that I *really* wanted to know. Emotional and spiritual need combined with urgency and humility to finally prepare me to receive what the Lord had in store for me.

In time, when the testimony came, it was powerful, simple, and beautiful. In the four decades that have passed since then, my testimony has enabled me to stay on the path walked by those trying their faltering best to become true disciples of Jesus Christ.

In the end, the strength, power, and validity of the Book of Mormon rests on one thing only: the convincing power of the Holy Ghost to the hearts of those who read it. Once received, that testimony is eternally enough. To those who never receive it, no amount of convincing will ring true.

> **The short answer:** "First, you're right—like many stories in the Holy Bible, it *is* a remarkable story, and I don't blame you for being cautious. I believe it because I've read the Book of Mormon from cover to cover, and I've asked the Lord to tell me if it is true or not. And it's hard to put things like this into words, but I know that God answered my prayers. Because of that I know that the Book of Mormon is a true book of scripture and is a second witness of Jesus Christ. Would you like a copy to read?

## SCRIPTURE SUPPORT:

| | |
|---|---|
| 1 Corinthians 2:14 | Spiritual things can only be discerned through the Spirit |

| Moroni 10:3–5 | The truthfulness of all things will be made manifest to you by the power of the Holy Ghost |
| Doctrine and Covenants 9:8 | First we must study and ponder, then ask if it be right; only then will the Spirit testify to us |

### Question #48: Isn't it wrong to have another book like the Holy Bible?

There are many who believe that the Holy Bible contains every word God intends to say to man and that to introduce anything more constitutes grave doctrinal heresy. From that perspective, our claim of modern scripture undermines the truth and authority of God, and it is therefore either misguided or evil.

Meanwhile, Latter-day Saints have no concern about modern-day scripture—as long as it comes from inside the Church. Anything from outside our faith claiming to be scripture would undermine the truth and authority of God and would therefore be of either misguided or evil origin.

In reality, our position is not that different from many other Christian churches. We come to them claiming new scripture and revelation given from God, and then we are surprised when they don't welcome us in like a long-lost relative. But if the situation was reversed, we would have the same reaction.

Nevertheless, our basic position that God continues to communicate with man not only through personal revelation but also through added scripture can certainly be defended.

From time to time, I've encountered the argument put forward in Revelation 22:18—"If any man shall add unto [this book], God shall add unto him the plagues that are written in this book." Many Christians suggest that John's comment, coming as it does at the end of our modern Bible, is made in reference to the entire Bible.

This is, however, a weak argument. The book of Revelation was written long before other writings we have in the Bible. This is understood and accepted by both LDS and non-LDS biblical scholars. If John meant to close all Christian scripture with his verse, then we would have neither the Gospel of John or any of his epistles.[89]

It's clear that at the time prophets and apostles were writing the things of God they never considered divine revelation to be finished. The Holy Bible itself was compiled over centuries. The arguments of 2 Nephi 29 ring true today:

---

89    There is no universal agreement of the exact year each book of the New Testament was written, but there is strong consensus of their general chronological order. The book of Revelation is considered to be written about fifteen years before the Gospel of John and twenty years before John's epistles. See, for example, the non-LDS website biblestudytools.com.

- God created all men, not just those in the Holy Land, and He loves them all equally.
- New scripture that testifies of Christ becomes another witness of His divinity.
- Additional scripture proves God is the same yesterday, today, and forever.
- His work is not and will never be finished.
- His words will be shared among all men for the benefit of mankind and His glory.[90]

The reality of modern scripture is a cornerstone of the Restoration of the gospel of Jesus Christ. When we present the idea, we must do it wrapped in the gift of God's love of mankind and not as an intellectual curiosity or additional commandment to be obeyed. Only then can our friends sense this great gift of the restored gospel for what it is—proof of a loving Father who has never left and will never leave His children without direction, love, or hope.

> **The short answer:** "The Holy Bible was compiled over centuries—it was never considered to be 'finished' in its day. We think it makes perfect sense that a loving Heavenly Father would continue to bless His children with ongoing scriptural revelation. Would you like a copy to read?"

## SCRIPTURE SUPPORT:

| | |
|---|---|
| 2 Nephi 29 | The entire chapter supports the idea of additional scripture |
| John 10:16 | Other sheep I have, which are not of this fold |
| Ezekiel 37:16–19 | The stick of Judah (the Bible) and the stick of Joseph (the Book of Mormon) will be made one |

---

90   The rationale of the Lord in 2 Nephi 29:7–13 is so logical that those who deny it must deny the love of God for all His children.

**Question #49: Haven't there been some changes made in the Book of Mormon through the years?**

A major claim of those who oppose divine authority of the Book of Mormon is that the book has been "changed thousands of times." They imply that the Church has attempted to cover up alleged deficiencies in the original manuscript by removing doctrinal and narrative faults and discrepancies. But facts point in a different direction.

During the translation process, Joseph spoke the words out loud, and his various scribes (mostly Oliver Cowdery) wrote them down. Joseph did not provide punctuation advice during the translation process. He did not say, for example, "I *comma* Nephi *comma* having been born of goodly parents . . ." He simply dictated the words. The lack of punctuation was a challenge for the typesetter of the first edition, John Gilbert, who was not a member of the Church. During the printing process, he inserted more than 30,000 punctuation marks to the original edition.[91]

Other changes reflect the difficulty of hearing something and being correct in writing it down. The words *straight* and *strait* would sound the same to the ear. Each time either word was used in the Book of Mormon, Oliver wrote down *straight*. Later editions required ten changes of *straight* to *strait* to convey the correct meaning.[92]

The Book of Mormon as originally found on the plates was not broken down into chapters and verses, although the designation of books existed. Chapter headings did not exist. And, of course, there were no study aids and cross references. All of these have been added over time

---

91   See George Horton, "Understanding Textual Changes in the Book of Mormon," *Ensign*, December 1983.

92   Ibid. This article contains a great deal of fascinating information about the development of the modern text of the Book of Mormon and the challenges facing typesetters through the years.

through early and later editions.[93] Spelling has also been modernized. *Steadfastly* was once spelled *stedfastly*, for example. The Church has not hidden these changes, and information about them can be easily found.[94]

As a result, the idea of a cover-up of these changes is simply not true. Critics who complain of changes in the Book of Mormon attempt to judge early printing efforts by modern standards. It is easy from our twenty-first century viewpoint to forget that in the early 1800s spelling was often a loose affair and printing techniques came nowhere close to modern standards. In no way have the changes to the Book of Mormon altered the doctrine or spiritual direction of this sacred text.

> **The short answer:** "The earliest editions of the Book of Mormon had revisions in spelling and punctuation. Back in 1981 and again in 2013, the Church issued new editions of the Book of Mormon with a lot more study helps. In each edition some of the word construction and spelling have been modernized, and minor punctuation errors were corrected from older editions."

## SCRIPTURE SUPPORT:

Mormon 9:31          Condemn not imperfections

---

93  There were four editions of the Book of Mormon during Joseph Smith's lifetime. The second, third, and fourth all contained improved spelling and punctuation. The fourth edition was published in England and included British spelling—*colour* for *color*, etc. The first attempt at dividing the book into verses (as opposed to paragraphs) didn't come until a British 1952 edition edited by Franklin D. Richards. It wasn't until 1879 that Orson Pratt oversaw an edition with shorter chapters and verses. The 1920 edition edited by James E. Talmage moved the text presentation forward significantly, with modern chapter headings, double columns and extensive cross-referencing. This edition of the Book of Mormon remained essentially unchanged until the 1981 edition, which revised chapter headings and fully integrated the Book of Mormon with other scriptures in the Topical Guide. The 1981 edition also introduced the expanded name of the Book of Mormon, adding the phrase "Another Testament of Jesus Christ" to the title. (All this information is taken from the *Encyclopedia of Mormonism* found at byu.edu/index, Book of Mormon Editions 1830–1981). In 2013 the Church introduced a new edition of the Book of Mormon with further revision of chapter headings and significantly expanded study aids.

94  See, for example, the article on adjustments made to the 2013 edition of the scriptures at lds.org/scriptures/adjustments.

### Question #50: So what's in the Book of Mormon that makes it special?

This question comes from a variety of directions, but they all make the same basic point: "Okay, so you've got this thing called the Book of Mormon. So what? Why do you care? Why should I?"

In the Church, we believe that the Book of Mormon restores many plain and precious things lost through the Apostasy, the translation process of the original scriptural manuscripts, and the simple weight of time.[95] Moreover, the entire tone of the book is more plain, meaning more easily understood. You can read the entire Book of Mormon and understand it. This is not a small thing.[96]

It is the book's accessibility that sets it apart from other books of scripture. Its doctrines are clear and so simple even a child can understand, a fact borne out each week in Primary as children speak with surprising maturity about the plan of salvation—who they are, where they came from, why they're here, and where they're going.

When I am asked what makes the Book of Mormon unique or special (other than its existence), I first respond with the fact that the Book of Mormon is so easy to understand. Then I share a verse or two that really mean something to me. I've listed a few below, but you'll always do better when you share a verse or doctrine that has touched *your* life or expanded *your* faith in a meaningful way.

> **The short answer:** "The Book of Mormon is special because it provides easy-to-understand guidance that brings us closer to Christ and helps us deal with life's problems. It tells about the coming of Jesus Christ to the Americas after His death and Resurrection. It is a beautiful book. Can I share with you a few of my favorite verses?"

The following are a few of my own favorite verses from the Book of Mormon:

---

95  For a concise and excellent summary of eight great scriptural truths restored in the Book of Mormon, see Clyde J. Williams, "Plain and Precious Truths Restored," *Ensign*, October 2006.

96  Consider this idea from President John Taylor: "It is true intelligence for a man to take a subject that is mysterious and great in itself and to unfold it and simplify it so that a child can understand it" ("Discourse," *Deseret News*, September 30, 1857, p. 238). One of the great blessings of the Book of Mormon is its ability to present doctrines in such understandable simplicity.

*We talk of Christ.* 2 Nephi 25:26

A former stake president of mine once suggested that if you only had time to share one verse from the Book of Mormon with someone, this would be a very good choice.

> We talk of Christ, we rejoice in Christ, we preach of Christ, we prophesy of Christ, and we write according to our prophesies, that our children may know to what source they may look for a remission of their sins.

*Weak things can become strong.* Ether 12:27

The idea that we can overcome our weakness and become stronger with God's help is not new, but it is presented here with such simple clarity that it can touch many formerly unreachable souls.

> And if men come unto me I will show unto them their weakness. I give unto men weakness that they may be humble; and my grace is sufficient for all men that humble themselves before me; for if they humble themselves before me, and have faith in me, then will I make weak things become strong unto them.

*Men are that they might have joy.* 2 Nephi 2:25

One short sentence that rocked my world as an investigator. In fourteen simple words, the fall of man, the mission of the Savior, and my purpose in all of it came to me in sudden laser-sharp focus. In a heartbeat I went from confusion to understanding.

> Adam fell that men might be; and men are, that they might have joy.

*Young children do not need baptism.* Moroni 8:11–12

An example of a plain and precious truth restored through the Book of Mormon and one of special comfort to parents. (For a more complete discussion, see verses 8–20.)

> And their little children need no repentance, neither baptism. Behold, baptism is unto repentance to the fulfilling the commandments unto the remission of sins.
>
> But little children are alive in Christ, even from the foundation of the world; if not so, God is a partial God, and also a changeable God, and a respecter to persons; for how many little children have died without baptism!

*The Atonement of Christ enables us to overcome all pain and suffering.*
Alma 7:11

A straightforward but soul-expanding view of the Atonement that reaches far beyond the Resurrection and forgiveness of sin, promising healing for all of life's wounds—both the seen and unseen.

> And he shall go forth, suffering pains and afflictions
> and temptations *of every kind*; and this that the word
> might be fulfilled which saith he will take upon him the
> pains and the sicknesses of his people. (italics added)

*His grace is sufficient.* Moroni 10:32

A beautiful verse that helps our friends understand why Mormons are committed to a life of active discipleship even though we believe it is only through the grace of Jesus Christ that we can be saved.

> Yea, come unto Christ, and be perfected in him, and
> deny yourselves of all ungodliness; and if ye shall deny
> yourselves of all ungodliness, and love God with all your
> might, mind and strength, then is his grace sufficient for
> you, that by his grace ye may be perfect in Christ; and
> if by the grace of God ye are perfect in Christ, ye can in
> nowise deny the power of God.

*Moroni's promise.* Moroni 10:4–5

To our friends who are not members of the Church, these are possibly the most important two verses in the Book of Mormon.

> And when ye shall receive these things, I would
> exhort you that ye would ask God, the Eternal Father,
> in the name of Christ, if these things are not true; and if
> you shall ask with a sincere heart, with real intent, having
> faith in Christ, he will manifest the truth of it unto you,
> by the power of the Holy Ghost.
>
> And by the power of the Holy Ghost ye may know
> the truth of all things.

# PART 3
## WISE AS SERPENTS, HARMLESS AS DOVES[97]

## A TIME TO SPEAK, A TIME TO KEEP SILENCE[98]

---

97    Matthew 10:16
98    Ecclesiastes 3:7

UP TO NOW WE'VE BEEN focused on giving accurate but short answers to basic gospel questions, but there are times when the short answers won't work. Sometimes the questions are just too big. Other times the questions are tipped with venom. For the next few pages, we'll focus on those moments when more is required. We will also deal with the challenge of how to respond when we find ourselves being attacked for our beliefs.

The too-big questions are often asked innocently, and the questioner doesn't realize he's swimming out to the deep end of the pool. I gave an example of this in Question #10: "Do you believe you are all going to become gods?" President Lorenzo Snow's statement, "As man is God once was, and as God is man may become," is powerful doctrine, but it is easy to distort and misunderstand. Sometimes you need to slow things down and delay a short, immediate answer so you can give a longer, deeper answer later. You may also want to delay giving an answer so that you can do a little more research yourself and perhaps even arrange to have someone else with you when you respond.

Questions that require this kind of approach might address many topics:

- The Apostasy: why the early Christian church lost its priesthood authority and why the Protestant Reformation wasn't sufficient to correct the problem, etc.
- The coming forth of the Book of Mormon: the recovery of the plates, the Angel Moroni, the translation process, etc.
- Deeper questions about the Church's stand on social issues: homosexuality, the relationship of women and the priesthood, abortion, etc.
- Some aspect of Church history that you don't know a lot about.

So if you're asked direct questions about these or other deeper topics, I suggest the following response: "That's a great question. Unfortunately, it's going to need more time to answer than we have right now. If you're really interested, we could talk about it later when we both have more time. When would work for you?"

The key phrase in this question is *if you're really interested.* This requires your friend to declare himself. Some will decline, and you can wrap things up with a sincere, "Well, thanks for asking; if you ever change your mind or have any other questions, I hope you'll ask."

But if they say they would like to continue the conversation, you should always ask the follow-up question, "May I ask why you're interested?" Hopefully your friend is sincerely interested in learning about the gospel, but it's possible he's asking so that he can draw you into an argument.

When you sense the question is just a prelude to a contentious debate, what do you do? As always, we can look to the Savior for the perfect example. In Matthew 10, the Savior called his Twelve Apostles and gave them instruction as they begin their apostolic ministry. His words are sobering: "Behold, I send you forth as sheep in the midst of wolves: be ye therefore wise as serpents, and harmless as doves" (Matthew 10:16).

Sometimes (but not often) "wolves" will seek to trap us in our words, to argue without the Spirit, to belittle our beliefs, and to condemn us for our testimonies. They will attempt to tell us what we believe and pounce on our slightest stumble as evidence of errant doctrine. Such experiences are hopefully few and far between, but when they occur I offer the following simple advice: STOP THE CONVERSATION AND LEAVE. Nothing good comes from what the missionaries call Bible bashing.

"Oh, yeah?" we argue. "I'll take your Ephesians 2:8 and raise you James 2:18. Take that!"

This is no way to win friends, and it won't enlighten anyone. The Spirit, if it was ever there, is long gone. It is replaced by anger and frustration. The goal becomes to score points against the other person—a textbook definition of pride, regardless of the theoretical nobility of the cause. These prideful confrontations happen on both sides of the argument.

Remember Ecclesiastes: there is "a time to every purpose under the heaven . . . a time to keep silence, and a time to speak" (Ecclesiastes 3:1, 7).

We need to be able to sense (or perhaps *feel* is the better word) the difference. Knowing when it is time for us to speak up about the gospel and when it is time to remove ourselves from situations in which the Spirit will not be present is part of what the Savior meant when he told his Apostles to be "wise as serpents, and harmless as doves" (Matthew 10:16).

We are harmless as doves when we respond with love to the earnest and well-meaning questions of others, respecting their questions, their agency, and their bravery for asking. In this setting our answers will be a blessing in their lives.

But there are occasionally times when we feel the Spirit's quiet voice telling us that at *this* moment with *this* individual the best blessing for all concerned is for us to keep silence about sacred things. Following that prompting will make us wise as serpents.

## BE READY ALWAYS TO GIVE AN ANSWER (1 PETER 3:15)

It is our privilege and blessing to live lives that radiate the power and goodness of the gospel. When we do, others will occasionally be drawn to us and seek to discover the source of our inner light. With the rare exceptions noted previously, it is a tender mercy from God when we are given the chance to answer sincere questions about our faith. We should seek to live so that, like Peter, we can "be ready always to give an answer to every man that asketh you a reason of the hope that is in you with meekness and fear" (1 Peter 3:15).

Often in the Church, we hear people pray that God will bless the missionaries that they will be lead to the honest in heart and those who are seeking the truth. I believe it will be a great day in the Church when we begin to pray that *we* will be lead to the honest in heart and those seeking the truth. And then, as we go through our days, we will try to see those we meet as God sees them, with a spirit clothed in the glory it received in the premortal world, and we will wonder—is this the one I have prayed to meet?

Perhaps if we were to make such an attempt, questions about the gospel would come to us more frequently.

By now you understand that the first question your friend asks is rarely the question that is actually on his mind. It's a test to see what kind of an answer you'll provide. If we earn our friend's trust with our response, then he may choose to ask a second or third question, which will inevitably reveal to us (and possibly even to himself) his own heart.

This is when we can understand what he *really* wants to know. And in the end there will always be unspoken questions that hang in the air: Does all of this make a difference in your life? Does it make you happier? More at peace with others? More at peace with yourself?

In all but the briefest discussions about the gospel with others, we should try and answer the unspoken question in whole or in part with the following messages:

- We (Mormons) are Christians who belong to a Christian church.
- I am trying my best to live the way Jesus wants me to.
- Around the world there are 15 million other Mormons who are trying to do the same thing.
- I am glad to belong to this Church. It helps me feel at peace and happy even in hard times.
- The Church is more than just a spiritual blessing in my life. It is a practical help to me as well.

This may sound like a lot to include in a gospel conversation, but it won't be difficult if your first question moves into an honest discussion. In my opinion, these basic points are worth committing to memory. Even in those rare times when you may find your beliefs under attack, this is the way you can withdraw with honor and dignity: You can tell those who choose confrontation that you are a Christian who belongs to a Christian church, that you are doing your best to live the Lord's commandments, that around the world millions of others share your beliefs, and that you are proud and happy to be a member of a Church blessed with the Holy Spirit of peace and charity towards others.

Others may nitpick our doctrine, but they can do nothing to touch your testimony.

# COME AND SEE (JOHN 1:39, 45–46)

IN THE END, ALL MISSIONARY work in the Church comes down to three words: *come and see.* Let me show you the beautiful way this works.

In John, the phrase "come and see" occurs twice in the first chapter in two very different settings. In the first, the Savior talks with two sincere men seeking light from the Master:

> Jesus turned, and saw them following, and saith unto them, What seek ye? They said unto him, Rabbi, . . . where dwellest thou?
>
> He saith unto them, Come and see.[99]

Then, a few verses later comes the same idea in a different setting:

> Philip findeth Nathanael, and saith unto him, We have found him, of whom Moses in the law, and the prophets, did write, Jesus of Nazareth, the son of Joseph.
>
> And Nathanael said unto him, Can there any good thing come out of Nazareth? Philip saith unto him, Come and see.[100]

In the first, humble followers ask to draw closer to the Savior. In the second, a man mocks with sarcasm the idea of the Savior coming from an insignificant, two-bit town like Nazareth. And yet, both receive the same answer.

Come and see.

Those words can give hope to the humble and deflate the sarcastic. "Don't take my word for it. Come and see for yourself. Put actions behind your words. Then you can properly draw your own conclusions."

---

99  John 1:38–39
100  John 1:45–46

The invitation to come and see is the beating heart of missionary work everywhere in the world. We invite others to come and see for themselves what the gospel of Jesus Christ has to offer. The rest is between them and God.

This book is about brevity—short answers to basic questions that may (or may not) lead to longer questions later. But in the end, the shortest answer of all, only three words long, may be the best answer to nearly every question.

Come and see.

Come and see what we have in The Church of Jesus Christ of Latter-day Saints.

Come and see the light that fills the eyes and hearts of those who have received the gift of the Holy Ghost.

Come and see people from all races and walks of life worshipping together.

Come and see families bound by temple covenants for time and all eternity.

Come and see men and women all pitching in to serve as teachers, helpers, and counselors with no thought of personal reward except the inner glow that comes from selfless service.

Come and see children who, with a wisdom unknown to many who are much older, will tell you where they came from before they were born, why they are here on earth, and where they are going after this life.

Come and see people giving freely of their time to help others in need, whether those who receive help are members of our Church or not.

Come and see friendship, love, and order coming together to bless all mankind.

Come and see what we have in The Church of Jesus Christ of Latter-day Saints.

And I'll be glad to sit beside you when you do.

# ABOUT THE AUTHOR

CHRIS HUSTON AND HIS WIFE Barbara joined the Church as newlyweds in 1973. Though never serving a mission, he recently served for three years as a counselor in the mission presidency of the Mississippi Jackson Mission. His experience on both sides of missionary work—as a once-struggling investigator and later as a missionary trainer—has given him a unique perspective on what works (and what doesn't) in sharing the gospel.

Professionally, Chris has spent thirty-five years in broadcast journalism as a reporter, anchor, and newsroom manager. He and his wife are the proud parents of eleven children and a rapidly growing crop of grandchildren. Currently he resides in southern Idaho.